SAMSUNG GALAXY WATCH 6
USER GUIDE

Unlocking the Full Potential of Your
Smartwatch and Essential Features You
Should Know

AARON P. BONNER

COPYRIGHT

TABLE OF CONTENTS

INTRODUCTION

The Samsung Galaxy Watch 6 is not just another smartwatch; it's an all-in-one device designed to streamline your life, improve your fitness, and elevate your overall health management. Whether you're looking to stay connected, monitor your health in real-time, or track your fitness goals with precision, the Galaxy Watch 6 is equipped with features that make it more than just a timepiece—it's an essential tool that integrates seamlessly into your daily routine.

In this guide, we will walk you through everything you need to know to get the most out of your Galaxy Watch 6. From the unboxing experience to setting up and personalizing your device, you will gain a comprehensive understanding of how this smartwatch can work for you, enhancing every aspect of your life.

Overview of the Watch

Samsung Galaxy Watch 6 Models: Standard and Classic

The Samsung Galaxy Watch 6 comes in two distinct models: the **standard Galaxy Watch 6** and the **Galaxy Watch 6**

Classic. Both models share the same core features but differ in design and style.

- **Galaxy Watch 6 Standard**: Sleek, modern, and minimalist, the standard model features a smooth, circular AMOLED display that fits seamlessly on your wrist. It offers a fresh, contemporary aesthetic that makes it suitable for both casual and formal occasions.

- **Galaxy Watch 6 Classic**: For those who prefer a more traditional and timeless look, the Classic model reintroduces the **rotating bezel**, a feature that many Samsung fans have longed for since it was removed in previous models. This mechanical bezel allows for a tactile, intuitive navigation experience, making it the perfect option for users who value the old-school charm of a classic watch face.

Design, Features, and Improvements Over Previous Models

The Galaxy Watch 6 is a powerful blend of cutting-edge technology and classic design, offering significant improvements over its predecessors. Let's break down some of the key upgrades and features:

- **Display**: The Galaxy Watch 6 comes equipped with a **Super AMOLED** display, offering vibrant colors and sharp resolution. Both models feature **sapphire crystal protection** for added durability, ensuring that your screen remains scratch-resistant and pristine. The Always-On Display feature means you can glance at the time or other key metrics without having to wake up the watch.

- **Performance**: Powered by the new **Exynos W930 processor**, the Galaxy Watch 6 runs faster and more efficiently than ever before. It offers smooth navigation, quick app launches, and the ability to manage multiple tasks at once. Coupled with **2GB of RAM** and **16GB of internal storage**, this smartwatch delivers top-tier performance.

- **Battery Life**: Samsung has made significant strides in optimizing battery life. With up to **40 hours of battery life** on a single charge, the Watch 6 can last through long days of work, workouts, and play without needing a recharge. For users who rely on features like the Always-On Display, the watch offers **30 hours** of usage, ensuring it's up to the task.

- **Health and Fitness Tracking**: One of the standout features of the Galaxy Watch 6 is its **advanced health monitoring** capabilities. Equipped with sensors for **ECG** (electrocardiogram), **blood pressure monitoring**, **blood oxygen saturation (SpO2)**, and **body composition analysis**, it's a complete health-tracking powerhouse. For fitness enthusiasts, it offers **over 90 workout modes**, including tracking for running, cycling, yoga, and swimming, with a built-in **GPS** for outdoor activities.

- **Connectivity**: The Galaxy Watch 6 is designed for seamless connectivity with your smartphone and other devices. It supports **Bluetooth 5.3**, **Wi-Fi** (2.4 GHz & 5 GHz), and **optional LTE** for users who want to go phone-free and still remain connected.

- **Durability**: The Galaxy Watch 6 is rated **5ATM** for water resistance, making it perfect for swimming and wearing in the rain. Additionally, it meets the **MIL-STD-810G** military standard for durability, meaning it's built to withstand harsh conditions.

Importance of Smartwatches in Daily Life and Health Management

Smartwatches, like the Galaxy Watch 6, have become indispensable in modern life, particularly when it comes to health management. These devices don't just tell time—they track your physical activity, monitor your health, and provide notifications that help you stay connected to the world around you.

With the increasing focus on personal health and wellness, smartwatches have evolved to offer features that monitor heart rate, stress levels, sleep quality, and more. The Galaxy Watch 6 takes these features a step further by providing real-time data and actionable insights. Whether you're tracking your heart rate during a workout, checking your sleep patterns, or keeping an eye on your blood pressure, the Watch 6 can help you make more informed decisions about your health.

Moreover, for those with busy lifestyles, the Galaxy Watch 6 helps you stay connected without having to reach for your phone. You can take calls, send texts, check emails, and access apps directly from your wrist, all while maintaining a sleek and stylish look.

Unboxing the Device

What's in the Box?

Opening the box for the first time is always an exciting experience. Here's what you can expect:

- **Samsung Galaxy Watch 6**: The star of the show, beautifully designed and ready to wear.

- **Charging Cable**: A **USB-C charging cable** designed for fast charging. The charging pad is wireless, meaning no need to plug the watch in directly.

- **User Manual**: A quick-start guide and user manual that will help you navigate your way through the initial setup and features.

- **Additional Accessories**: Depending on the package or region, some boxes may also include additional straps or watch faces to personalize your experience.

Initial Setup Steps

The setup process for the Galaxy Watch 6 is designed to be as simple as possible. Here's how you can get started:

1. **Powering On**: Hold down the **power button** on the side of the watch to turn it on. You'll see the Samsung logo appear, followed by the initial setup screen.

2. **Pairing with Your Phone**: To get the most out of your Galaxy Watch 6, you'll need to pair it with your smartphone. Download the **Galaxy Wearable app** from the Google Play Store or Apple App Store, depending on your device. Open the app and follow the on-screen instructions to pair your phone with the watch via **Bluetooth**.

3. **Account Setup**: Once paired, you will be prompted to sign in with your **Samsung account**. If you don't have one, it's easy to create one. This account will allow you to access Samsung's ecosystem, including apps and services like **Samsung Health**.

4. **Connecting to Wi-Fi**: If you plan on using apps and features that require an internet connection, make sure to connect your watch to a Wi-Fi network during setup.

5. **Customizing the Watch**: After setup, you can start customizing your watch face, changing settings like

vibration and brightness, and adjusting the overall look and feel of the device.

Getting Familiar with the Device

Once your Galaxy Watch 6 is set up and ready to go, it's time to explore. Here are some key elements to familiarize yourself with:

- **The Touchscreen**: The AMOLED display on the Galaxy Watch 6 is a beauty to behold, offering bright, vibrant colors and an intuitive interface. Tap to access apps, swipe for notifications, and pinch to zoom in on certain details.

- **Rotating Bezel (Classic Model)**: If you opted for the Classic model, the rotating bezel is a major highlight. Use it to scroll through apps, adjust settings, and navigate without touching the screen.

- **Buttons and Controls**: The **Home button** (bottom button) takes you back to the home screen or app drawer. The **Back button** (top button) helps you return to the previous screen.

- **Fitness and Health Features**: Explore the **Samsung Health** app to see your daily activity, set fitness goals, track your workouts, and monitor your health metrics in real-time.

- **Quick Settings**: Access quick settings like Wi-Fi, Do Not Disturb, and battery-saving mode with a swipe down from the top of the screen.

- The Samsung Galaxy Watch 6 is much more than a timepiece—it's an essential companion that helps you stay connected, track your health, and manage your day-to-day activities with ease. Whether you're looking to enhance your fitness routine, keep an eye on your heart health, or simply streamline your daily tasks, the Galaxy Watch 6 offers a comprehensive set of tools to make your life more efficient.

From the unboxing experience to mastering the device's many features, this guide will ensure you have everything you need to make the most of your Samsung Galaxy Watch 6. As you explore the watch's many capabilities, you'll quickly see that it's not just about style; it's about empowering you to live smarter, healthier, and more connected. Enjoy your journey with your new Samsung Galaxy Watch 6, and unlock all the possibilities it has to offer!

CHAPTER 1

Getting Started with Your Samsung Galaxy Watch 6

The Samsung Galaxy Watch 6 is a powerful device designed to enhance your productivity, health management, and overall convenience. With its sleek design, customizable features, and extensive functionality, it's a perfect blend of style and technology. This chapter will guide you through everything you need to know to get started, from pairing your watch with your smartphone to navigating its interface and customizing it to fit your preferences.

Setting Up Your Watch

When you first unbox your Samsung Galaxy Watch 6, the setup process is straightforward and intuitive. Whether you're new to Samsung devices or upgrading from an older model, this step-by-step guide will walk you through pairing your Galaxy Watch 6 with your smartphone, installing essential apps, and syncing your devices to maximize your smartwatch experience.

Pairing Your Samsung Galaxy Watch 6 with Your Smartphone (Android and iOS)

One of the first things you'll need to do is pair your Galaxy Watch 6 with your smartphone. Whether you're using an Android device or an iPhone, pairing the two devices will enable you to sync notifications, apps, and settings. Here's how you can do it:

For Android Users:

1. **Download the Galaxy Wearable App**: The first step is to download and install the **Galaxy Wearable** app from the **Google Play Store**. The app is free and works seamlessly with your Samsung Galaxy Watch 6.

2. **Enable Bluetooth on Your Phone**: Make sure that Bluetooth is enabled on your smartphone. You'll need this for the watch to connect to your phone.

3. **Turn on Your Watch**: Press and hold the **Power button** on the right side of the Galaxy Watch 6 to power it on.

4. **Open the Galaxy Wearable App**: Open the Galaxy Wearable app on your phone. The app will

automatically search for nearby devices. Select your Galaxy Watch 6 from the list.

5. **Confirm Pairing**: A pairing request will pop up on your phone and watch. Confirm the request on both devices to pair them.

6. **Sync Your Devices**: Once paired, the app will begin syncing your Galaxy Watch 6 with your smartphone. You'll be prompted to set up your watch's preferences and sync notifications, apps, and settings.

For iPhone Users:

1. **Download the Galaxy Watch 6 App**: Since the Galaxy Wearable app is designed primarily for Android devices, iPhone users will need to download the **Samsung Galaxy Watch 6 app** from the **App Store**.

2. **Enable Bluetooth on Your iPhone**: Make sure Bluetooth is turned on for easy pairing.

3. **Power On the Galaxy Watch 6**: Press and hold the **Power button** to turn the watch on.

4. **Open the Galaxy Watch 6 App**: Launch the Galaxy Watch 6 app, and the app will scan for nearby devices.

5. **Select Your Watch**: Once your Galaxy Watch 6 appears on the app, select it to start the pairing process.

6. **Confirm Pairing**: A confirmation window will appear on both your iPhone and the Galaxy Watch 6. Confirm the pairing on both devices to complete the connection.

After pairing your devices, the setup process will guide you through additional configurations like connecting to Wi-Fi, setting up Samsung accounts, and syncing data.

Installing the Galaxy Wearable App

To make the most out of your Samsung Galaxy Watch 6, you will need to install the **Galaxy Wearable** app on your smartphone. The Galaxy Wearable app is the central hub for managing your watch, installing new apps, syncing notifications, and customizing settings.

Installing the App on Android:

1. Open the **Google Play Store** on your Android phone.

2. Search for **Galaxy Wearable** in the search bar.

3. Tap **Install** and wait for the app to download and install.

4. Open the app once it's installed and follow the on-screen instructions to complete the pairing process.

Installing the App on iOS:

1. Open the **App Store** on your iPhone.

2. Search for **Samsung Galaxy Watch 6** (or Galaxy Wearable).

3. Tap **Get** to download the app.

4. After installation, open the app and follow the prompts to sync your watch.

Once installed, the Galaxy Wearable app will allow you to adjust settings, track your fitness goals, and manage the apps installed on your watch.

Setting Up an Account and Syncing Your Devices

After pairing your Samsung Galaxy Watch 6 with your phone, you'll need to create or sign in to your **Samsung Account**. This account enables you to access Samsung services, including Samsung Health, Samsung Pay, and other apps.

Creating a Samsung Account:

1. Open the **Galaxy Wearable app**.

2. If you don't already have a Samsung account, you'll be prompted to create one.

3. Tap **Create Account** and follow the prompts to enter your details, including email, password, and security information.

4. After successfully creating your account, sign in to complete the setup.

Once logged in, the Galaxy Wearable app will automatically sync your Galaxy Watch 6 settings with your Samsung account, ensuring that your data is backed up and accessible across all your devices.

Navigating the Interface

The Samsung Galaxy Watch 6 comes with a user-friendly interface that blends touch controls, physical buttons, and for the Classic model, a rotating bezel. Whether you are navigating the touchscreen, pressing buttons, or rotating the bezel, understanding these features will enhance your smartwatch experience. In this section, we'll explore how to use all the input methods and customize the interface to your liking.

Understanding the Touchscreen, Physical Buttons, and Rotating Bezel (For the Classic Model)

The Samsung Galaxy Watch 6 offers a seamless navigation experience through its combination of a touchscreen, physical buttons, and, for the Classic model, the rotating bezel. Here's how each method works:

Touchscreen:

The touchscreen is your primary method for interacting with the Galaxy Watch 6. Whether you're scrolling through apps, responding to notifications, or swiping to check your health data, the touchscreen provides a responsive and intuitive interface.

- **Tap**: Use tapping gestures to open apps, select options, or activate widgets.

- **Swipe**: Swipe up, down, left, or right to navigate between apps, view notifications, or access the quick settings menu.

- **Pinch**: You can pinch to zoom in or out of maps and photos.

Physical Buttons:

The Galaxy Watch 6 is equipped with two physical buttons on the right side of the device. These buttons are used for navigation and powering the watch on or off.

- **Power Button (Bottom Button)**: This is the primary button for powering the watch on and off. It also returns you to the main screen from any app or menu.

- **Back Button (Top Button)**: The back button allows you to return to the previous screen or navigate backward in an app.

Rotating Bezel (Classic Model Only):

The rotating bezel on the Classic model is one of the most loved features by Samsung users. This feature provides a tactile, hands-on navigation experience that allows you to scroll through menus, adjust settings, and navigate without touching the screen.

- **Scroll**: Rotate the bezel to scroll through apps, settings, or notifications.

- **Select**: Click the bezel to select an option when the desired item is highlighted on the screen.

Using the Home Button, Back Button, and Power Button

Understanding how to use the buttons is essential for smooth navigation. Here's what each button does:

- **Home Button**: The home button (the bottom button on the right side) takes you to the main screen or the home page of your watch. Press it once to return to the home screen from any app or menu.

- **Back Button**: The back button (the top button) allows you to navigate backward. If you're deep within a menu or app, press it to go back to the previous screen.

- **Power Button**: The power button is used for powering the watch on or off. To power on the device, press and hold the power button. To turn off the watch, press and hold the button again until the option to turn off appears on the screen.

- **Pressing and Holding the Power Button**: Press and hold the power button to bring up the power menu, which gives you options like restarting the watch or turning it off.

Customizing the Watch Face

One of the first things you'll want to do when setting up your Galaxy Watch 6 is customize the watch face. With a variety of built-in options and the ability to download third-party faces, the watch face can reflect your personal style, preferences, and functionality needs.

Choosing a Watch Face:

1. **Long-press the Watch Face**: To access the watch face selection screen, long-press on the current watch face.

2. **Browse Pre-installed Watch Faces**: Scroll through the available pre-installed watch faces, ranging from simple analog clocks to complex digital ones with added information.

3. **Download New Faces**: Tap **Galaxy Store** to explore and download additional watch faces. There are numerous free and premium options available, offering everything from minimalist designs to interactive, data-rich layouts.

Customizing the Watch Face:

Once you've selected a watch face, you can customize it further:

1. **Complications**: Choose the information you want to display on the watch face. This can include heart rate, weather, calendar events, step count, and more.

2. **Colors and Styles**: Depending on the watch face you choose, you can customize its colors, styles, and layout to match your preferences.

3. **Interactive Elements**: Some watch faces allow for interactive elements, where tapping certain areas will open apps or display additional data.

The Samsung Galaxy Watch 6 is a state-of-the-art smartwatch that combines cutting-edge technology with sleek design. Setting up and navigating the watch is straightforward, even for those who are new to the world of smartwatches. By following the steps outlined in this chapter, you will be able to pair your watch with your smartphone, navigate through its interface with ease, and customize it to suit your needs.

With the **Galaxy Wearable app**, you can maximize your smartwatch experience, stay connected, and manage your health effectively. The combination of the touchscreen, physical buttons, and the rotating bezel (on the Classic model) ensures that you have the flexibility to interact with the watch in the way that feels most natural to you. Whether you're checking your health metrics, customizing your watch face, or managing notifications, the Galaxy Watch 6 provides a versatile and user-friendly experience.

In the next chapters, we'll dive deeper into exploring the advanced features of the Galaxy Watch 6, from health and fitness tracking to connectivity and app integration. Stay tuned for an in-depth look at how to get the most out of your Samsung Galaxy Watch 6!

CHAPTER 2

Personalizing Your Experience with the Samsung Galaxy Watch 6

One of the most exciting aspects of owning a Samsung Galaxy Watch 6 is the ability to personalize the device to suit your individual style, preferences, and needs. The Galaxy Watch 6 is designed to be a highly customizable smartwatch, offering users the ability to tailor everything from the watch face to the notifications and display settings. Personalizing your watch allows you to make it truly yours, ensuring that it fits seamlessly into your daily routine, whether you're using it for health tracking, managing notifications, or simply checking the time. This chapter will guide you through the process of customizing your watch, including choosing and adjusting watch faces, personalizing notifications, and optimizing the display for comfort and convenience.

Choosing and Customizing Watch Faces

The watch face is one of the most important elements of your Galaxy Watch 6. Not only does it tell the time, but it also serves as an expression of your personal style. Whether you prefer a sleek, minimalistic design or a more data-driven interface with various complications, there's a watch face for you. Samsung offers a variety of watch faces that come pre-installed, and you can also download third-party faces for even more customization. Let's explore the process of choosing and customizing watch faces to match your unique style.

Selecting a Watch Face that Fits Your Style and Needs

When setting up your Samsung Galaxy Watch 6 for the first time, one of the first things you'll want to do is select a watch face. Your choice of watch face can say a lot about your personality and the functionality you want from the device. There are many options available, ranging from analog and digital designs to more complex watch faces that include multiple data points.

Here's how to select a watch face:

1. **Long-Press the Current Watch Face**: To access the watch face selection menu, press and hold the current watch face on your screen. This action will trigger a gallery of available watch faces that you can scroll through.

2. **Browse Available Watch Faces**: You'll see a variety of built-in watch faces to choose from. These can range from simple, minimalistic designs to feature-rich, complex faces that display additional information such as the weather, your heart rate, or the date.

3. **Choose a Watch Face**: Once you've found a watch face that catches your eye, tap it to select it. You can swipe left or right to explore different designs, styles, and layouts that suit your personal aesthetic.

4. **Set as Default**: After selecting a watch face, it will become your default, but you can always change it again later if you find something else you like better.

How to Customize Colors, Complications, and Layout

After selecting a watch face, many of them can be customized further. Whether you're looking to change the color scheme, add complications, or adjust the layout, you have plenty of options. Complications are additional data points that can be displayed on the watch face, such as heart rate, step count, weather, and more.

Here's how to customize your watch face:

1. **Long-Press on the Watch Face**: Again, long-press on the watch face that's currently displayed on your Galaxy Watch 6.

2. **Tap on Customize**: When the customization options appear, tap on the **Customize** button to start making changes.

3. **Change the Color Scheme**: Many watch faces offer color adjustments. You can change the background color or text color to match your personal style. Some watch faces may offer multiple color schemes, giving you the flexibility to select the one that fits your mood or outfit for the day.

4. **Add or Remove Complications**: Depending on the complexity of the watch face, you can add different complications to display more data points. Tap on the complication section, and you'll be able to choose from options like:

   o **Weather**: Display the current temperature and forecast.

   o **Heart Rate**: Show your current heart rate at a glance.

- Activity/Steps: Keep track of your daily steps or calories burned.

- Battery Life: Display the remaining battery percentage.

You can also remove any complications that you don't find useful, ensuring that the watch face remains clean and uncluttered.

5. **Adjust Layout**: Some watch faces allow you to modify the layout or rearrange elements. If you want to prioritize certain data points or adjust the placement of your complications, this is where you can make those changes.

Using Third-Party Watch Faces from the Galaxy Store

While the pre-installed watch faces offer a wide variety of options, Samsung's **Galaxy Store** provides even more customization through third-party apps. These apps allow you to access hundreds of additional watch faces, many of which offer unique designs or enhanced functionality that may not be available in the default set.

Here's how to download and use third-party watch faces:

1. **Open the Galaxy Store**: From your Samsung Galaxy Watch 6, swipe up to access the apps menu and tap on **Galaxy Store**. If you haven't already installed the store, you can download it from the **Galaxy Wearable app** on your phone.

2. **Browse Watch Faces**: In the Galaxy Store, tap on the **Watch Faces** category to view the available options. You'll see both free and paid options. Some watch faces may require an in-app purchase or subscription.

3. **Download and Install**: Once you find a watch face you like, tap on it to download and install it. Once it's installed, it will appear in your list of available watch faces in the **Galaxy Wearable app**.

4. **Apply the New Watch Face**: After installing the watch face, it will automatically appear in your list of options. Simply go back to your watch, long-press the current watch face, and select the new one to apply it.

Adjusting Settings for Comfort

Now that you've customized your watch face, it's time to personalize the settings for comfort and functionality.

Samsung Galaxy Watch 6 offers a wealth of customization options to adjust notifications, vibrations, display brightness, and more. These settings ensure that the watch is not only a stylish accessory but also a highly functional device tailored to your needs.

How to Personalize Notifications, Do Not Disturb Mode, and Sounds

The notifications on your Galaxy Watch 6 are one of its most important features. Whether you're getting a call, a text message, or an app notification, you want to make sure they're received in the most convenient way possible.

Here's how to personalize your notifications:

1. **Customizing Notifications**: Open the **Galaxy Wearable app** on your phone, then tap on **Notifications**. Here, you can choose which apps will send notifications to your watch. You can select from messaging apps, social media platforms, emails, calendar reminders, and more.

2. **Setting up Do Not Disturb Mode**: If you need some quiet time, you can use the **Do Not Disturb** mode. To enable this, swipe down on the watch screen to access the quick settings, then tap on the **Do Not**

Disturb icon (a circle with a line through it). This will silence all notifications and calls.

3. **Sound Settings**: From the **Galaxy Wearable app**, tap on **Sound and Vibration**. You can adjust the volume of notifications and set different sound profiles for various times of the day, such as when you're at work or sleeping.

Setting Up Haptic Feedback and Vibration Intensity

One of the key features of the Galaxy Watch 6 is the ability to receive notifications through haptic feedback. This allows you to feel vibrations on your wrist when you receive a notification or alert, which is especially useful when you're in noisy environments or during workouts.

Here's how to adjust the vibration settings:

1. **Haptic Feedback**: In the **Sound and Vibration** section of the **Galaxy Wearable app**, you can turn on or off the haptic feedback for notifications, calls, and alerts.

2. **Vibration Intensity**: You can adjust the strength of the vibration under the **Vibration Strength** option in the **Galaxy Wearable app**. Choose a low, medium,

or high setting depending on how strong you want the vibrations to be.

3. **Vibration Pattern**: Some users prefer different vibration patterns for different types of alerts. In the **Vibration Pattern** settings, you can choose a short vibration, long vibration, or a repeated pattern.

Adjusting Brightness, Always-On Display, and Other Display Settings

The display is one of the standout features of the Samsung Galaxy Watch 6. With its Super AMOLED screen, it's vibrant and clear, but it's also highly customizable to match your preferences. Adjusting the brightness and enabling the Always-On Display can help you ensure the screen is always visible when you need it.

Here's how to adjust the display settings:

1. **Brightness**: Swipe down from the top of the screen to open the quick settings menu. From there, tap on **Brightness** to adjust the screen brightness. You can set it to auto-adjust based on ambient light, or manually set it to a level that suits your needs.

2. **Always-On Display**: To enable the Always-On Display, go to **Settings** > **Display** > **Always On**

Display. This feature will keep the time and select data visible even when the watch is not in use, which is convenient if you need to quickly glance at the time.

3. **Sleep Mode**: If you prefer a dimmer screen during the night, you can enable **Sleep Mode**. This feature dims the display and disables notifications to help you get a more restful night of sleep. You can enable it through the **Quick Settings** or schedule it through **Settings** > **Display** > **Sleep Mode**.

4. **Screen Timeout**: You can set the screen timeout duration to control how long the screen stays active after interacting with the watch. This is done under **Settings** > **Display** > **Screen Timeout**. Choose from options like 15 seconds, 30 seconds, or 1 minute.

Customizing your Samsung Galaxy Watch 6 is a simple and enjoyable process, allowing you to tailor the device to fit your personal style, preferences, and lifestyle needs. From selecting the perfect watch face to adjusting notifications and vibration settings, the Galaxy Watch 6 offers an abundance of personalization options that make it truly yours.

With the ability to customize everything from the display settings to the watch face layout, you'll have complete control over how your smartwatch looks, feels, and functions. Whether you're focused on health tracking, staying connected, or just enjoying the aesthetics, the Galaxy Watch 6 can be personalized to meet all your needs.

As you explore and adjust these settings, you'll soon realize how much more enjoyable and functional your Galaxy Watch 6 can become. So, take the time to experiment with different options, try out various watch faces, and set your preferences to make your smartwatch a powerful extension of yourself. Enjoy the process of making the Galaxy Watch 6 uniquely yours!

CHAPTER 3

Advanced Health Features on the Samsung Galaxy Watch 6

The Samsung Galaxy Watch 6 is not just a stylish smartwatch—it's also a powerful health tool that can help you track and manage key aspects of your well-being. With advanced health features like ECG (electrocardiogram), blood pressure monitoring, sleep tracking, and body composition analysis, the Galaxy Watch 6 is designed to provide you with real-time data to help you understand your health better and make informed decisions. In this chapter, we will explore the advanced health features of the Galaxy Watch 6, focusing on heart health, sleep monitoring, and body composition analysis. By the end of this section, you'll be equipped with the knowledge to make the most of these features and take charge of your health.

Tracking Your Heart Health

Monitoring your heart health is one of the most important aspects of using a smartwatch, and the Galaxy Watch 6 takes it to the next level with its advanced ECG functionality, blood pressure monitoring, and heart rate zone tracking during workouts. These features help you stay informed about your heart's condition and ensure that you're maintaining an active and healthy lifestyle.

How to Use ECG for Monitoring Heart Rhythms

An electrocardiogram (ECG) is a medical test that measures the electrical activity of the heart. The ECG feature on the Samsung Galaxy Watch 6 allows you to monitor your heart rhythm directly from your wrist, providing insights into your heart's health. This feature is particularly useful for detecting signs of irregular heart rhythms, such as atrial fibrillation (AFib), which can lead to serious complications if left untreated.

Setting Up and Using the ECG Feature:

1. **Install the ECG App**: First, ensure that the ECG app is installed on your Galaxy Watch 6. The app should be pre-installed, but if it isn't, you can download it from the **Galaxy Store** through the **Galaxy Wearable app**.

2. **Pair with Your Phone**: Make sure your watch is paired with your smartphone via the **Galaxy Wearable app**. The app is essential for syncing the ECG data with your phone.

3. **Prepare to Take an ECG**: To use the ECG function, sit down in a comfortable position. Ensure that you are wearing your watch snugly on your wrist and that it is clean and dry. It's best to take an ECG when you're relaxed and calm, as stress can affect heart rate readings.

4. **Take the ECG**: To start the ECG, open the **ECG app** on your watch and follow the on-screen instructions. You'll be asked to place your finger on the **top button** of the watch (the power button). The device will then measure your heart's electrical activity. The process usually takes about 30 seconds.

5. **View Your Results**: After the ECG test is completed, you'll see your results on the watch's screen. The watch will provide a report indicating whether it detected normal sinus rhythm or if it found any irregularities, such as AFib. If irregularities are detected, you'll be advised to consult with a healthcare provider for further evaluation.

6. **Store Your Results**: The ECG data will be stored in the **Samsung Health Monitor app** on your phone, where you can review past tests and share the results with your doctor if necessary.

Setting Up and Using Blood Pressure Monitoring

In addition to the ECG feature, the Galaxy Watch 6 includes a **blood pressure monitoring** function, allowing you to measure your blood pressure directly from your wrist. This is a valuable feature for individuals who need to keep track of their blood pressure regularly, especially those at risk for hypertension.

Setting Up Blood Pressure Monitoring:

1. **Install the Samsung Health Monitor App**: The blood pressure monitoring feature works in conjunction with the **Samsung Health Monitor app**. If you don't have the app installed, download it from the **Galaxy Store** and set it up on your phone.

2. **Calibrate the Watch**: Before using the blood pressure feature, you must calibrate your watch with a traditional cuff-based blood pressure monitor. This ensures that your readings are accurate. To calibrate, you will need to take at least two measurements using a cuff-based device and input the results into the **Samsung Health Monitor app**.

3. **Measuring Blood Pressure**: To measure your blood pressure, open the **Samsung Health Monitor app**

on your Galaxy Watch 6 and select the **Blood Pressure** option. Sit down in a relaxed position and make sure your wrist is at the level of your heart. Follow the on-screen instructions to take the reading, which usually takes a minute or so.

4. **Review Your Results**: After the measurement is complete, you will see your systolic and diastolic pressure readings. The results are also saved in the Samsung Health Monitor app, where you can track changes in your blood pressure over time.

5. **Consulting Your Healthcare Provider**: If your blood pressure readings are consistently high, it's important to consult a healthcare provider. The Galaxy Watch 6's blood pressure monitoring feature can help you stay informed about your cardiovascular health, but it should not be used as a replacement for professional medical care.

Tracking and Analyzing Heart Rate Zones During Workouts

Heart rate monitoring is an essential part of any fitness routine, as it allows you to track your intensity levels and ensure that you're working out at the optimal level for your fitness goals. The Galaxy Watch 6 allows you to monitor your heart rate in real-time during workouts and provides insights into your heart rate zones.

Understanding Heart Rate Zones:

Heart rate zones are ranges of heart rates that indicate different levels of exercise intensity. These zones can help you target specific fitness goals, such as burning fat or improving cardiovascular endurance. The common heart rate zones are:

- **Zone 1 (Very Light)**: 50-60% of maximum heart rate

- **Zone 2 (Light)**: 60-70% of maximum heart rate

- **Zone 3 (Moderate)**: 70-80% of maximum heart rate

- **Zone 4 (Hard)**: 80-90% of maximum heart rate

- **Zone 5 (Maximum)**: 90-100% of maximum heart rate

The Galaxy Watch 6 tracks your heart rate during workouts and assigns you to one of these zones based on your current heart rate. This allows you to ensure that you're staying within your target zone for the desired outcome.

Tracking Heart Rate Zones:

1. **Start a Workout**: Open the **Samsung Health app** and select the workout mode you're about to engage in, such as running, cycling, or swimming.

2. **Monitor Your Heart Rate**: During your workout, the watch will display your heart rate in real-time. The heart rate will be color-coded to correspond to the zone you're in (e.g., green for Zone 2, yellow for Zone 3).

3. **Post-Workout Insights**: After completing your workout, the Galaxy Watch 6 provides detailed data on your heart rate zones, including how much time you spent in each zone, the average heart rate, and the total duration of your workout.

Sleep Tracking and Insights

Getting enough quality sleep is essential for maintaining overall health and well-being. The Samsung Galaxy Watch 6's advanced sleep tracking feature can help you monitor your sleep patterns, assess sleep quality, and offer recommendations for improvement. In this section, we'll explore how to set up and use the sleep tracking feature, analyze your sleep data, and make the most of the sleep coach function.

Setting Up Sleep Monitoring

Before you can begin tracking your sleep with the Galaxy Watch 6, you need to enable the sleep monitoring feature in the **Samsung Health** app. Follow these steps to set up sleep tracking:

1. **Open the Samsung Health App**: On your Galaxy Watch 6, open the **Samsung Health** app and scroll down to find the **Sleep** section.

2. **Enable Sleep Tracking**: Tap on **Sleep** to enable the sleep tracking feature. If you're using the feature for the first time, you may be prompted to complete a short setup process, including adjusting settings like notification preferences and syncing your watch with the app.

3. **Wear Your Watch to Sleep**: For the most accurate results, wear your Galaxy Watch 6 while you sleep. Make sure the watch is snug on your wrist and comfortable enough that it won't disturb your sleep.

4. **Track Sleep Data**: The Galaxy Watch 6 will automatically detect when you fall asleep and begin

tracking your sleep cycles. It will record data on your total sleep duration, sleep stages (light, deep, and REM sleep), and any interruptions that occur throughout the night.

Analyzing Your Sleep Patterns: Sleep Stages, Quality, and Tips for Improvement

Once you wake up, the Galaxy Watch 6 will provide you with detailed insights into your sleep patterns. You can review your sleep data in the **Samsung Health app**, which provides an in-depth look at your sleep stages, quality, and any disturbances.

Sleep Stages:

- **Light Sleep**: The lighter stage of sleep where your body is still processing information, but you're not fully restful.

- **Deep Sleep**: The most restorative stage of sleep, where the body heals and regenerates.

- **REM Sleep**: The stage where dreaming occurs and the brain consolidates memories and emotional processing.

Sleep Quality:

The watch tracks not only the total duration of your sleep but also the quality, including how long you spent in each stage. Poor sleep quality can indicate that you're not getting enough deep or REM sleep, which is crucial for recovery.

Improvement Tips:

If the data shows that your sleep quality is poor, the Galaxy Watch 6 offers tips for improving it. These may include suggestions for maintaining a consistent bedtime, reducing screen time before sleep, or engaging in relaxation techniques.

Using the Sleep Coach Feature to Optimize Your Rest

The **Sleep Coach** feature on the Galaxy Watch 6 offers personalized insights and recommendations based on your sleep data. It uses your sleep patterns to create tailored suggestions for improving the quality and duration of your sleep.

How to Use the Sleep Coach:

1. **Access the Sleep Coach**: Open the **Samsung Health app** on your phone and navigate to the **Sleep** section. Here, you'll find personalized recommendations.

2. **Review Sleep Data**: The app will provide a summary of your sleep data, including your sleep score (a rating based on the quality of your sleep), the total amount of sleep you got, and any disruptions.

3. **Follow Recommendations**: Based on your sleep data, the Sleep Coach will provide suggestions for improving your sleep. These might include setting a consistent bedtime, practicing relaxation techniques before sleep, or eliminating sleep distractions.

Body Composition Analysis

The Samsung Galaxy Watch 6 provides an advanced **Body Composition Analysis** feature, allowing you to track metrics such as body fat percentage, muscle mass, and other vital health indicators. Understanding these metrics is essential for overall health and fitness, as they give you a deeper insight into your body's composition beyond weight alone.

How to Track Body Fat, Muscle Mass, and Other Vital Metrics

Body composition is a key indicator of your overall health. Rather than just focusing on weight, understanding how much of your body is composed of fat, muscle, and water gives you a more accurate picture of your fitness and health.

Using the Body Composition Analysis Feature:

1. **Activate the Feature**: Open the **Samsung Health app** on your Galaxy Watch 6 and navigate to **Body Composition**.

2. **Input Personal Information**: To get accurate results, you'll need to input some personal details, such as your age, gender, and height.

3. **Measure Your Body Composition**: Hold your wrist still for a few moments while the watch performs the analysis. It uses bioelectrical impedance analysis (BIA) to measure resistance in your body tissues, estimating fat mass, muscle mass, and other body metrics.

4. **Review Your Results**: After the measurement, you'll see your body fat percentage, muscle mass, bone mass, and other health data. These metrics will be saved in the Samsung Health app, where you can track your progress over time.

Understanding the Importance of Body Composition for Overall Health

Unlike weight, which can fluctuate due to factors like water retention or muscle gain, body composition gives a more reliable indication of your health and fitness levels. Here's why it matters:

- **Body Fat**: Too much body fat, especially visceral fat (fat stored around organs), can lead to health problems like heart disease, diabetes, and high blood pressure.

- **Muscle Mass**: Maintaining or increasing muscle mass is important for metabolism, strength, and overall fitness.

- **Bone Mass**: Healthy bones are essential for mobility and long-term health, especially as you age.

Tips on Improving Your Health Based on Body Composition Data

1. **Adjust Your Diet**: If your body fat percentage is high, focus on improving your diet by eating nutrient-dense foods like vegetables, lean proteins, and whole grains. Cutting back on processed foods and sugars can help lower body fat over time.

2. **Strength Training**: To increase muscle mass, include resistance training or weightlifting in your routine. Building muscle not only boosts metabolism but also supports joint health and bone density.

3. **Stay Hydrated**: Water plays a crucial role in the body composition process, so make sure to stay well-hydrated to improve overall health metrics.

4. **Track Progress**: Regularly check your body composition data to see improvements or areas that need attention. Consistency is key in reaching your health and fitness goals.

The Samsung Galaxy Watch 6 is an exceptional tool for monitoring and improving your health. With its advanced health features—ECG, blood pressure monitoring, heart rate tracking, sleep monitoring, and body composition analysis—the watch offers a comprehensive way to manage your well-being. Whether you're tracking your heart health, improving your sleep, or gaining insights into your body composition, the Galaxy Watch 6 equips you with the tools needed to take control of your health journey.

By understanding how to use and interpret these advanced health features, you'll be better prepared to make informed decisions about your lifestyle, fitness, and overall health. Keep tracking, stay motivated, and make the most of the Samsung Galaxy Watch 6 to lead a healthier, more balanced life.

CHAPTER 4

Fitness and Exercise Tracking on the Samsung Galaxy Watch 6

The Samsung Galaxy Watch 6 is not just a smartwatch—it's a fitness powerhouse designed to help you stay active, monitor your progress, and reach your fitness goals. Whether you're a casual walker, an experienced runner, a cyclist, or someone who practices yoga, the Galaxy Watch 6 provides comprehensive fitness tracking tools to keep you on track. With an extensive range of exercise modes, advanced fitness features, and detailed post-workout insights, this device empowers you to monitor your performance and make data-driven decisions for your health. In this chapter, we will dive into the various exercise modes, the advanced features that make your workouts more effective, and how to analyze your workout data to optimize your fitness journey.

Exercise Modes Overview

One of the standout features of the Samsung Galaxy Watch 6 is its ability to track a wide range of exercise modes, catering to virtually every type of workout. Whether you're into running, cycling, swimming, or yoga, this smartwatch has you covered. Each exercise mode is designed to provide real-time metrics and insights, so you can track your performance and make improvements based on accurate data.

A List of Exercise Modes Available on the Watch

The Galaxy Watch 6 supports a comprehensive set of exercise modes to suit various fitness activities. Some of the most popular exercise modes include:

1. **Running**: This is one of the most commonly used modes for tracking outdoor runs. It provides metrics such as distance, pace, heart rate, and calories burned. The watch also tracks splits, lap times, and average pace to help you monitor your running performance.

2. **Cycling**: Whether you're on a stationary bike or cycling outdoors, the Galaxy Watch 6 provides a cycling mode that tracks your distance, cadence, heart rate, and calories burned. For outdoor cycling, the GPS tracking feature is also enabled to help you map your route.

3. **Yoga**: This mode is designed for tracking activities like stretching, breathing, and yoga poses. The watch

monitors your heart rate, calories burned, and time spent in different poses. While the Galaxy Watch 6 doesn't track every yoga pose individually, it provides a good overall measure of your workout.

4. **Swimming**: With its **5ATM water resistance**, the Galaxy Watch 6 is suitable for swimming in the pool or open water. The swimming mode tracks your lap count, stroke type, distance swum, and stroke efficiency. It also tracks heart rate while you swim, providing a comprehensive view of your swimming workout.

5. **Walking**: Similar to running, the walking mode tracks your distance, pace, heart rate, and calories burned, but it's more suited for slower-paced walking activities. It also provides detailed step count data and offers insight into your walking cadence.

6. **Hiking**: For those who love hiking outdoors, the Galaxy Watch 6 features a hiking mode that tracks elevation gain, distance, and route, utilizing the built-in GPS for real-time mapping and route guidance.

7. **Strength Training**: Whether you're lifting weights, doing bodyweight exercises, or using resistance bands, the strength training mode helps track sets, reps, and calories burned. The watch will also monitor your heart rate during strength-based exercises.

8. **Rowing**: If you enjoy rowing, the Galaxy Watch 6 tracks your rowing stroke rate, distance, and calories burned. It's an ideal mode for those who row on machines or in open water.

9. **HIIT (High-Intensity Interval Training)**: HIIT training is all about short bursts of intense exercise followed by rest periods. The Galaxy Watch 6 supports this mode by tracking interval times, heart rate, and calories burned, allowing you to optimize your HIIT sessions.

10. **Other Exercise Modes**: The Galaxy Watch 6 also supports additional workout modes such as dancing, golf, pilates, tennis, and more. Each mode tracks essential data specific to that activity.

How to Start and Stop a Workout

Getting started with a workout on the Samsung Galaxy Watch 6 is simple. Here's how you can begin tracking your exercise:

1. **Start a Workout**:

   o **Swipe Up** on the watch face to access the apps menu.

   o Tap the **Samsung Health app** to open the workout section.

   o Browse through the available exercise modes or search for your specific workout (e.g., running, cycling, swimming).

   o Select the exercise mode you want to use, and the watch will immediately begin tracking.

   o If you're engaging in an outdoor activity (like running or cycling), the GPS will automatically activate to track your route.

2. **Stop a Workout**:

   o When you're ready to stop the workout, press the **Back button** or swipe the screen to pause the session.

   o Tap the **Stop** button, and the watch will display a summary of your workout stats.

   o You can save your session or discard it if you prefer.

Customizing Workout Settings for Personalized Tracking

The Galaxy Watch 6 allows you to tailor your workout tracking settings to match your preferences. You can adjust various aspects of the workout modes, such as heart rate zones, alerts, and data display.

1. **Customize Data Display**:

   o Open the **Samsung Health app** and select the exercise mode you want to adjust.

   o Tap **Settings** and select the **Data Display** option. Here, you can choose which data fields to display during your workout, such as pace, heart rate, distance, and calories burned.

2. **Set Heart Rate Zones**:

   o   To ensure you're working out at the optimal intensity, you can customize your heart rate zones. Go to the **Heart Rate Zones** setting and input your maximum heart rate, resting heart rate, and target zones. The watch will notify you when you reach certain zones during your workout.

3. **Enable Alerts**:

   o   For specific workout modes, you can set **alerts** for when you reach certain thresholds, such as a specific heart rate, pace, or distance. These alerts help you stay focused on your goals and prevent overexertion.

Advanced Fitness Features

The Samsung Galaxy Watch 6 offers advanced fitness features that go beyond simple step counting and calorie tracking. With tools like VO2 Max, pace, distance, cadence tracking, and GPS, the watch provides athletes and fitness enthusiasts with the detailed metrics they need to monitor and improve their performance. Let's explore these advanced features in more detail.

Tracking VO2 Max, Pace, Distance, and Cadence

1. **VO2 Max**:

    o **What It Is**: VO2 Max is a measure of your body's ability to consume oxygen during exercise. It's considered one of the best indicators of cardiovascular fitness and endurance.

    o **How to Track It**: The Galaxy Watch 6 uses data from your heart rate, pace, and other metrics to estimate your VO2 Max during aerobic exercises like running and cycling. This data helps you track improvements in your aerobic capacity over time.

    o **Where to Find It**: After completing a workout, you can view your VO2 Max reading in the **Samsung Health app**. It will also provide insights into whether you're improving your fitness level.

2. **Pace**:

   o **What It Is**: Pace refers to how quickly you're moving, typically measured in minutes per mile or minutes per kilometer.

   o **How to Track It**: During running or cycling sessions, the Galaxy Watch 6 provides real-time pace data, helping you monitor your speed and intensity. The watch will display your average pace, lap times, and fluctuations during your workout.

3. **Distance**:

   o **What It Is**: Distance is a key metric for tracking progress in outdoor workouts such as running, walking, and cycling.

   o **How to Track It**: Using the built-in GPS, the Galaxy Watch 6 tracks your exact route and calculates the total distance covered. Whether you're running around a track or cycling through the city, the watch will record your distance with precision.

4. **Cadence**:

   o **What It Is**: Cadence refers to the number of steps per minute (for running or walking) or revolutions per minute (for cycling).

   o **How to Track It**: The Galaxy Watch 6 tracks your cadence during your workout and provides insights into how efficient your movements are. By monitoring cadence, you can improve your stride length and overall running form.

Integrating Your Watch with Samsung Health and Third-Party Fitness Apps

The Galaxy Watch 6 seamlessly integrates with **Samsung Health**, offering a comprehensive overview of your fitness and health data. But the versatility doesn't end there— Samsung allows for integration with various third-party fitness apps, giving you even more flexibility to track your workouts.

1. **Samsung Health**:

   o The Samsung Health app acts as the hub for all your fitness data, including step count, calories burned, heart rate, and more. You can track progress over time, set goals, and view insights into your workouts.

o The app provides advanced features like weekly and monthly summaries, trend analysis, and fitness assessments.

2. **Third-Party Apps**:

o If you prefer other fitness tracking apps, the Galaxy Watch 6 is compatible with popular apps like **Strava**, **MyFitnessPal**, **Runkeeper**, and more.

o You can connect these apps through the **Galaxy Wearable app** to sync workout data, share information, and consolidate all your fitness metrics into one place.

o **Fitness Sync**: Many third-party apps offer syncing features with Samsung Health, ensuring that all your workout data is accessible in one location.

Using GPS for Outdoor Activities and Mapping Your Runs

One of the most valuable features for outdoor enthusiasts is the **GPS functionality**. Whether you're running through a park or cycling around your neighborhood, the Galaxy Watch 6's GPS capabilities allow you to map your route, monitor your pace, and track your progress in real-time.

1. **Start Your Workout**: When you select an outdoor exercise mode (such as running or cycling), the watch will automatically connect to the GPS to begin tracking your location.

2. **Map Your Route**: As you move, the watch records your exact route, showing your path on the map. This is especially useful for runners, hikers, and cyclists who want to revisit their favorite routes or discover new ones.

3. **Real-Time Data**: The watch continuously updates your distance, pace, and route as you move, allowing you to stay focused on your workout without constantly checking your phone or other devices.

Post-Workout Insights

After you complete a workout, the Galaxy Watch 6 provides detailed post-workout insights that help you assess your performance and plan your next steps. These insights include metrics like performance scores, recovery tips, and progress tracking, all of which are essential for improving your fitness levels.

How to Analyze Your Workout Data After Completion

Once you stop a workout, the Galaxy Watch 6 compiles a summary of your session, offering a detailed analysis of your performance. The data is synced with the **Samsung Health app**, where you can review your workout metrics in depth. Here's how to analyze your workout data:

1. **Workout Summary**: The app provides a breakdown of your key metrics, including:

   o **Time**: Total duration of your workout.

   o **Distance**: Total distance traveled (for running, cycling, walking).

   o **Heart Rate**: Your average and peak heart rate during the workout.

- o **Calories Burned**: The total number of calories you burned during the session.

2. **Performance Insights**: The app offers insights into your performance based on your fitness level, such as VO2 Max, pace, and cadence.

3. **Comparison**: The Samsung Health app can compare your latest workout data to previous sessions, helping you track progress and identify areas for improvement.

Understanding Performance Scores, Recovery Tips, and Progress Tracking

In addition to the basic workout data, the Galaxy Watch 6 provides performance scores, recovery tips, and progress tracking features:

1. **Performance Scores**: The Galaxy Watch 6 uses data from your workout to generate a performance score. This score takes into account your heart rate, pace, and other factors to give you an overall rating of your effort.

2. **Recovery Tips**: After a workout, the Galaxy Watch 6 provides recovery suggestions based on the intensity of your exercise. These tips may include

hydration recommendations, stretching, and rest periods.

3. **Progress Tracking**: Over time, the Galaxy Watch 6 tracks your performance metrics, allowing you to see trends and improvements. Whether you're tracking your running speed, strength training progress, or swimming distance, the watch helps you stay motivated and focused on your goals.

The Samsung Galaxy Watch 6 is a versatile and powerful fitness companion that offers everything you need to track your workouts, monitor your health, and improve your fitness performance. From the variety of exercise modes to advanced features like VO2 Max tracking, GPS, and post-workout insights, the watch is designed to support you on your fitness journey.

By understanding and utilizing the fitness and exercise tracking features, you can make more informed decisions about your workouts and health, ensuring that you're always on the right track. Whether you're a beginner or a seasoned athlete, the Galaxy Watch 6 provides the tools you need to reach your fitness goals and beyond. With its comprehensive data, advanced metrics, and easy-to-use interface, the Galaxy Watch 6 is more than just a watch—it's a fitness partner that helps you achieve success, one workout at a time.

CHAPTER 5

Using Connectivity Features on the Samsung Galaxy Watch 6

One of the standout features of the Samsung Galaxy Watch 6 is its seamless connectivity options. Whether you're pairing the watch with your smartphone, setting it up for standalone use with LTE, or integrating it with your smart home devices, the Galaxy Watch 6 offers versatility and convenience. Additionally, it allows you to make calls, send messages, and access real-time navigation through GPS and map features. In this chapter, we'll explore how to use these connectivity features to make the most of your Galaxy Watch 6, including how to pair it with your smartphone, set up LTE, and connect to other devices and services like SmartThings.

Connecting to Your Smartphone and Other Devices

The Galaxy Watch 6 is designed to sync effortlessly with your smartphone and other devices, allowing for a smooth and integrated experience. Whether you're using Bluetooth, Wi-Fi, or LTE, setting up these connections will enable you to access your notifications, control apps, and even make calls directly from your wrist. Let's break down how to connect your Galaxy Watch 6 to your smartphone and other devices.

Pairing via Bluetooth and Wi-Fi

The primary connection method for your Galaxy Watch 6 is **Bluetooth**, which allows the watch to sync with your smartphone and other devices. Additionally, the watch supports **Wi-Fi** connectivity, enabling you to stay connected when Bluetooth is out of range, such as when you're at the gym or a remote location.

Pairing via Bluetooth:

1. **Download the Galaxy Wearable App**: Start by downloading the **Galaxy Wearable** app from the Google Play Store or Apple App Store, depending on your phone's operating system.

2. **Enable Bluetooth on Your Phone**: Open the Bluetooth settings on your smartphone and ensure that Bluetooth is turned on.

3. **Power On Your Galaxy Watch 6**: Press and hold the **Power button** on the right side of your Galaxy Watch 6 to turn it on.

4. **Open the Galaxy Wearable App**: Once the app is installed on your phone, open it and follow the on-screen prompts to begin the pairing process. The app will automatically search for your Galaxy Watch 6.

5. **Select Your Watch**: When the Galaxy Wearable app detects your watch, it will appear in a list of available devices. Tap on your watch to initiate the pairing.

6. **Confirm Pairing**: A pairing request will appear on both your phone and watch. Confirm the pairing on both devices to establish the connection.

7. **Sync Your Devices**: After pairing, the app will sync your Galaxy Watch 6 with your phone. You'll be prompted to enable notifications, install updates, and set up any additional preferences.

Pairing via Wi-Fi:

1. **Connect to Wi-Fi**: On your Galaxy Watch 6, swipe down from the top of the screen to access the **Quick Settings** menu. Tap the **Wi-Fi icon** to enable Wi-Fi.

2. **Choose a Network**: Select your desired Wi-Fi network and enter the password if required. Once connected, your Galaxy Watch 6 will automatically stay connected to the Wi-Fi network.

3. **Stay Connected**: With Wi-Fi enabled, you can receive notifications, download apps, and sync data without needing to be in Bluetooth range of your phone.

Setting Up LTE (If Applicable) for Standalone Use

If you have the **LTE-enabled version** of the Galaxy Watch 6, you can use the watch independently of your smartphone. With an LTE connection, you can make and receive calls, send messages, and use data without needing to keep your phone nearby. Setting up LTE is simple, but you will need to have a **compatible mobile plan** with your carrier.

Setting Up LTE:

1. **Ensure Compatibility**: Check with your carrier to confirm that they support LTE for smartwatches and that you have the appropriate mobile plan.

2. **Activate LTE on Your Watch**: From the **Galaxy Wearable app** on your phone, go to the **Mobile Plans** section and select **Add Plan**. Follow the instructions provided by your carrier to activate LTE on your watch.

3. **Complete the Activation Process**: The carrier will provide a QR code that you need to scan with your

Galaxy Watch 6 to activate the connection. Once the activation is complete, your watch will have its own mobile data connection.

4. **Use LTE for Standalone Functionality**: With LTE set up, your Galaxy Watch 6 can function completely independently. You'll be able to make calls, send texts, and access apps using mobile data without needing to be connected to your phone.

Syncing with Other Smart Home Devices and Apps (SmartThings, etc.)

The Galaxy Watch 6 is designed to integrate with various smart home devices and apps, providing a connected experience that extends beyond fitness and communication. One of the key features of the Galaxy Watch 6 is its ability to sync with **Samsung's SmartThings** ecosystem, allowing you to control and monitor your smart home directly from your wrist.

Syncing with SmartThings:

1. **Install the SmartThings App**: Ensure you have the **SmartThings app** installed on your smartphone. This app will allow you to control compatible smart devices in your home.

2. **Connect Devices to SmartThings**: Open the SmartThings app on your phone and add your compatible smart devices, such as lights, thermostats, and security cameras. Follow the in-app instructions to pair each device.

3. **Sync with Your Watch**: Once your devices are connected to the SmartThings app, open the **Galaxy Wearable app** on your phone and go to the **SmartThings** section. Tap to sync your devices with the Galaxy Watch 6.

4. **Control Your Smart Home**: After syncing, you'll be able to control your smart devices directly from the **SmartThings app** on your watch. You can adjust the lights, thermostat, or lock doors, all from your wrist.

Third-Party App Integrations:

In addition to SmartThings, the Galaxy Watch 6 can integrate with various third-party apps like **Google Home**, **IFTTT**, and more. These integrations provide you with more flexibility and control over your smart home and other connected devices.

Making and Receiving Calls

One of the most convenient features of the Samsung Galaxy Watch 6 (especially with LTE) is the ability to make and receive calls directly from your wrist. Whether you're out for a jog, working in the garden, or just don't want to pull out your phone, this feature makes staying connected a breeze.

How to Make Calls Directly from the Watch (If LTE Enabled)

With LTE enabled, the Galaxy Watch 6 becomes a fully functional phone replacement, allowing you to make and receive calls without needing your smartphone nearby.

Making Calls:

1. **Open the Phone App**: Swipe up on the watch face to access the app menu and tap on the **Phone** app.

2. **Dial a Number**: You can either dial a number manually using the on-screen keypad or tap on the contacts to find a person you want to call.

3. **Use Voice Commands**: Alternatively, use the **Bixby** voice assistant or **Google Assistant** (if configured) to make a call hands-free. Just say something like,

"Hey Bixby, call [contact name]" or "Call [phone number]."

Receiving Calls:

1. **Incoming Call Alert**: When someone calls you, the Galaxy Watch 6 will ring, and the caller's information will appear on the screen.

2. **Answering a Call**: Tap the green **answer** button to pick up the call. You can speak directly into the watch's microphone and listen through the built-in speaker.

3. **Declining a Call**: If you don't want to take the call, simply swipe to decline, or you can send a message directly from the watch with a pre-written response.

Sending Text Messages, Using Voice Commands, and Dictation

In addition to making calls, the Galaxy Watch 6 lets you send text messages and emails using voice commands or the built-in keyboard.

Sending Text Messages:

1. **Open the Messages App**: Swipe up on the watch face, then tap on the **Messages** app.

2. **Create a New Message**: Tap the + button to start a new message, then select a contact.

3. **Type or Dictate**: You can use the **on-screen keyboard** to type your message, or tap the **microphone icon** to dictate your message. The watch will convert your voice to text, making it easier to reply on the go.

Using Voice Commands:

- **Bixby Voice Assistant**: With **Bixby**, you can dictate messages, set reminders, make calls, and control your watch entirely with voice commands. Simply activate Bixby by saying, "Hey Bixby" or by pressing and holding the power button.

- **Google Assistant**: If you prefer Google's assistant, you can use **Google Assistant** on the Galaxy Watch 6. Just say, "Hey Google" to activate it and give commands like sending messages or checking the weather.

Navigating with Maps and GPS

The Samsung Galaxy Watch 6 is equipped with a powerful GPS system that allows you to navigate through maps and track your outdoor activities with accuracy. Whether you're running, cycling, hiking, or simply exploring, the watch can help you find your way and monitor your progress in real time.

Using the Map Features for Navigation

The Galaxy Watch 6's built-in GPS allows you to access detailed maps and get turn-by-turn navigation without needing to pull out your smartphone. This feature is especially useful for runners, cyclists, or hikers who want to track their route and distance.

Navigating with Maps:

1. **Open the Maps App**: On your Galaxy Watch 6, swipe up to access the apps menu and open the **Maps** app.

2. **Search for a Location**: Enter the address or location you want to navigate to, or you can use voice commands to search.

3. **Start Navigation**: Once the location is selected, tap **Navigate** to start the directions. The watch will provide turn-by-turn instructions, and it will vibrate when it's time to make a turn.

Setting Up Location-Based Alerts

Location-based alerts are handy for outdoor activities like running, hiking, or cycling. The Galaxy Watch 6 can notify you when you reach certain locations, helping you stay on track.

1. **Set a Location Alert**: In the **Samsung Health app**, set up a location-based alert for when you reach a certain point on your route (e.g., a specific distance or landmark).

2. **Receive Notifications**: The watch will vibrate and send a notification when you've reached your destination or the preset location.

Tracking Your Runs, Hikes, and Outdoor Activities with GPS Precision

The GPS functionality of the Galaxy Watch 6 isn't just about navigation—it also tracks your location with pinpoint accuracy during outdoor activities. Whether you're running, hiking, or cycling, the GPS will map your route and provide valuable insights into your performance.

1. **Start a Workout**: When you begin a workout, such as running or hiking, the watch will automatically activate GPS to track your location.

2. **Track Your Route**: As you move, the watch will record your path and provide real-time updates on your distance, pace, and current location on a map.

3. **Review Your Data**: After completing your workout, you can review your route, performance stats, and even export your data to third-party apps like Strava for further analysis.

The Samsung Galaxy Watch 6 is a versatile and powerful smartwatch, providing a rich set of connectivity features that keep you connected to the world, whether you're at home, at work, or on the go. From pairing with your smartphone and setting up LTE for standalone use to controlling your smart home devices with SmartThings, the Galaxy Watch 6 integrates seamlessly into your daily life.

With its ability to make and receive calls, send messages, and navigate with precision using GPS, the Galaxy Watch 6 is more than just a timepiece—it's a comprehensive connectivity hub. As you explore all these features, you'll discover how the Galaxy Watch 6 can help you stay in touch, stay fit, and stay connected, no matter where life takes you.

CHAPTER 6

Battery Management and Performance Optimization on the Samsung Galaxy Watch 6

The Samsung Galaxy Watch 6 is a powerful smartwatch, packed with features designed to enhance your daily life, health tracking, and productivity. However, like all devices, its battery life can be influenced by how you use it. From constantly checking notifications to using GPS for outdoor workouts, the way you manage your watch's battery plays a significant role in keeping it running efficiently. In this chapter, we will delve into practical tips for maximizing the battery life of your Galaxy Watch 6, how to monitor battery health over time, and how to optimize performance for extended usage. Additionally, we will explain the various power modes and settings that can help conserve battery life when necessary.

Maximizing Battery Life

The Galaxy Watch 6 boasts impressive battery life, but, like any high-performance device, it can be drained quickly depending on how it's used. By tweaking some settings and using certain features wisely, you can extend the battery life significantly. Below are some key tips to help you maximize the battery life of your watch.

Battery-Saving Tips and Settings

Maximizing battery life on the Samsung Galaxy Watch 6 requires a combination of strategic settings adjustments and mindful usage. Here are some simple but effective tips that can help you get the most out of each charge.

1. **Disabling the Always-On Display (AOD)**:

    o   The **Always-On Display** (AOD) is a convenient feature that keeps your watch face visible at all times. However, this feature can significantly impact battery life. To conserve power, consider disabling the Always-On Display.

    o   To turn off AOD, swipe down from the top of the screen to access the **Quick Settings**. Tap the **AOD** icon to disable it, or go to **Settings > Display > Always On Display** and switch it off. This will prevent your watch face from staying lit continuously, thus saving battery.

2. **Reducing Background Apps**:

   ○ Background apps can use significant power by continually syncing data or running tasks. The Galaxy Watch 6 allows you to disable or limit background apps to save battery.

   ○ To adjust background app settings, go to **Settings > Apps > Manage apps** and disable apps that don't need to be running in the background. You can also turn off notifications for apps that you don't need to be alerted about constantly.

3. **Limiting Notifications**:

   ○ Constant notifications—whether from emails, social media apps, or messages—can drain the battery by keeping the screen active and consuming processing power. Limiting notifications to only the essential apps will help improve battery performance.

   ○ To manage notifications, go to **Settings > Notifications** and select which apps you want to receive alerts from. You can disable notifications for less important apps or choose to only receive critical alerts like calls and messages.

4. **Turning Off Vibration Alerts**:

   o Vibrations are an important part of the notification system on the Galaxy Watch 6, but they also consume battery. If you don't need vibrations for all notifications, consider turning them off.

   o To adjust vibration settings, go to **Settings > Sound and Vibration** and adjust vibration strength or turn off vibrations for certain types of notifications.

5. **Adjusting the Screen Brightness**:

   o The display is one of the most power-hungry components of the Galaxy Watch 6. Reducing the screen brightness can significantly improve battery life, especially if you are in a low-light environment.

   o To adjust brightness, swipe down from the top of the screen to open the **Quick Settings**. Tap the **Brightness** icon and slide it to a lower level. You can also go to **Settings >**

Display and manually set the brightness to the level that suits your needs.

6. **Use Power-Saving Watch Faces**:

    o   Some watch faces are designed to consume less power by using simple designs and static images. Opting for these power-saving faces can help you conserve energy while still enjoying the aesthetic of the watch.

    o   In the **Galaxy Wearable app**, you can select simpler watch faces that have fewer complications and less animation. These watch faces will use less power and extend your battery life.

How to Monitor Battery Health and Performance Over Time

Understanding how your battery is performing over time can help you make informed decisions about how to optimize battery usage. Monitoring battery health and usage patterns is important for ensuring that your Galaxy Watch 6 remains efficient over time.

1. **Battery Health and Usage Insights**:

   o The **Battery** section in the **Settings** menu provides insights into how much battery is being consumed by different apps and features. This allows you to identify which features are draining your battery the most.

   o To access this data, go to **Settings > Battery**. Here, you'll see a breakdown of your watch's battery usage, showing how much power is consumed by various apps, sensors, and services.

2. **Battery Performance Over Time**:

   o As with any battery-powered device, the battery performance of your Galaxy Watch 6 may degrade over time. Regularly checking your battery's health is a good practice.

   o Although Samsung does not provide a specific "battery health" indicator for the watch, you can gauge its performance by observing how long it lasts between charges. If you notice a rapid decline in battery life, it may be time to reassess your settings or check

85

for software updates that could optimize performance.

3. **Battery Optimization Tools**:

   o The **Samsung Wearable app** provides a tool to monitor the health of your Galaxy Watch 6's battery. The app gives an overview of how often the watch is charged and how quickly the battery drains. By monitoring this data over time, you can spot patterns and make adjustments accordingly.

Charging the Device: Methods and Recommended Practices for Optimal Battery Life

Proper charging practices can help ensure that your Galaxy Watch 6's battery lasts longer and continues to function optimally. Let's explore how to charge your device correctly and what practices can help optimize battery life.

1. **Charging the Galaxy Watch 6**:

   o The Galaxy Watch 6 uses **wireless charging**, which requires a **charging dock** or pad that comes with the device. Place your watch on the charging pad, ensuring that the charging pins on the watch align with the charging pad.

2. **Charging Time**:

   o Typically, the Galaxy Watch 6 takes about **1 to 2 hours** to fully charge. Charging it for a shorter period (e.g., 30 minutes to an hour) is usually sufficient to restore battery life for daily use.

3. **Avoid Overcharging**:

   o It's important not to overcharge the Galaxy Watch 6. While it's designed to handle continuous charging, it's always best to unplug it once it's fully charged to prevent strain on the battery.

4. **Charging Best Practices**:

   o If you're traveling or need a quick charge, consider **charging the watch intermittently** throughout the day rather than leaving it plugged in for long periods. This reduces stress on the battery and helps maintain its lifespan.

Understanding Power Modes

To further optimize battery life, the Galaxy Watch 6 offers several **power modes** that can be adjusted based on your needs. Whether you're traveling, working out, or simply trying to conserve battery, these modes allow you to customize performance and power usage.

Explanation of Power Saving and Low Power Modes

1. **Power Saving Mode**:

    o   Power Saving Mode is designed to extend battery life by turning off non-essential features while keeping core functions active. This mode reduces background app updates, dims the screen brightness, and limits notifications. It's particularly useful when you have low battery but need to keep the watch operational.

How to Enable Power Saving Mode:

o   Swipe down from the top of the watch screen to access the **Quick Settings**.

o   Tap the **Battery** icon and select **Power Saving**.

o You can choose **Low Power** or **Ultra Power Saving** mode depending on how much battery you want to conserve.

2. **Low Power Mode**:

   o Low Power Mode allows the watch to continue basic functions, such as timekeeping and fitness tracking, while minimizing power consumption. It turns off features like Always-On Display, reduces background syncing, and dims the screen.

How to Enable Low Power Mode:

   o Go to **Settings** > **Battery** and toggle on **Low Power Mode**. This will ensure that your watch remains functional while extending battery life over an extended period.

How to Adjust Settings to Conserve Battery During Long Trips or Workouts

When you're traveling or working out, your Galaxy Watch 6 can consume a lot of power due to GPS tracking, active sensors, and notifications. Adjusting certain settings during these activities can help conserve battery life.

1. **GPS and Location Tracking**:

   o When engaging in outdoor activities like running or hiking, GPS tracking can drain your battery quickly. To conserve energy, make sure to disable GPS when not needed.

   o If you only need GPS tracking for specific activities, turn off continuous location tracking and only use it when required.

2. **Workout Mode Adjustments**:

   o For long workouts, disable unnecessary features like Always-On Display and background app syncing. You can also lower the screen brightness and limit notifications to only the most important ones.

   o Access **Workout Settings** in the **Samsung Health app** and select only the necessary features for your exercise mode (e.g., heart rate tracking, distance, etc.).

Optimizing Performance During Travel or Extended Usage

When traveling or on long trips, battery conservation is key, especially if you are away from a charger for an extended period. The Galaxy Watch 6 offers several features that make it easy to manage performance and battery usage during these times.

1. **Switch to Power Saving Mode**:

   o For long trips, enable **Power Saving Mode** to minimize battery consumption. This mode ensures that essential functions, like timekeeping and basic fitness tracking, continue while conserving power.

2. **Turn Off Unused Features**:

   o Disable Wi-Fi, Bluetooth, and LTE when not in use. These connectivity features can consume a significant amount of power, especially when the watch is constantly searching for a connection.

3. **Reduce Background Apps**:

   o   Before heading out on a long trip, take some time to disable or limit the background apps on your watch. Apps like weather or social media notifications can drain the battery over time.

4. **Charge on the Go**:

   o   Consider carrying a portable **charging pad** or **power bank** during travel. This will ensure that you can top up your watch when necessary, especially during long days of sightseeing or business meetings.

Battery management and performance optimization are critical aspects of getting the most out of your Samsung Galaxy Watch 6. By using the tips and settings outlined in this chapter, you can maximize battery life, extend its lifespan, and ensure that your watch performs optimally for your needs. Whether you're looking to extend your watch's battery during a workout, while traveling, or for general everyday use, the Galaxy Watch 6 offers a wealth of settings to help you optimize power consumption.

With features like **Power Saving Mode**, **Low Power Mode**, and the ability to adjust screen brightness, notifications, and background apps, you have complete control over how your watch uses its battery. By adopting these strategies, you can keep your watch running for longer periods without constantly needing to recharge. Whether you're out for a run, traveling the world, or simply getting through a busy day, the Galaxy Watch 6 can be your constant companion without worrying about running out of battery.

CHAPTER 7

Security and Privacy Features on the Samsung Galaxy Watch 6

In today's interconnected world, protecting your personal information and maintaining privacy is essential. The Samsung Galaxy Watch 6 is equipped with advanced security and privacy features that help you safeguard your device, data, and personal information. From setting up a secure PIN or password to protecting your health and activity data, this smartwatch ensures that your sensitive information remains secure. This chapter will guide you through the steps of securing your Galaxy Watch 6, activating essential privacy settings, and understanding how Samsung handles your data to ensure both security and privacy.

Protecting Your Device

Your Samsung Galaxy Watch 6 is not just a timepiece but a powerful device that houses a wealth of personal information, including messages, emails, health data, and payment details. Protecting this information is a priority, and Samsung provides several methods to secure your device.

Whether you're concerned about unauthorized access or accidental loss, setting up proper security measures can significantly enhance the protection of your watch.

Setting Up a PIN, Pattern, or Password for Security

One of the first steps in securing your Samsung Galaxy Watch 6 is setting up a PIN, password, or pattern. This ensures that only you can access the watch and its data. Here's how to set up a security lock on your device:

Setting Up a PIN or Password:

1. **Open Settings**: From the watch face, swipe down to open the **Quick Settings**, then tap on the **Settings** icon (gear symbol).

2. **Navigate to Security**: Scroll down and select **Security**. This option will allow you to set up various types of security features, such as a PIN, password, or pattern.

3. **Choose Lock Type**: You'll be given the option to choose between a PIN, password, or pattern. Here's a breakdown of each option:

   o **PIN**: A simple numeric code (usually 4-6 digits) that you can easily memorize.

o **Password**: A more secure option where you can create an alphanumeric password for your watch.

o **Pattern**: A graphical pattern that you can draw on the screen to unlock your watch.

4. **Create Your Security Lock**: Choose the method that works best for you. If you select a PIN or password, you will be prompted to enter your preferred code or password. If you choose a pattern, you will be asked to draw a secure pattern on the screen.

5. **Confirm Your Choice**: Once you've set up your lock, you may be asked to confirm it by re-entering the PIN, password, or pattern to ensure it was set up correctly.

6. **Activate Lock Screen**: Once confirmed, the lock will be enabled, and you'll need to enter your chosen security method each time you access the watch. This ensures that no one can use your device without your permission.

Why a PIN or Password Is Essential:

Setting up a PIN or password is one of the most important steps in securing your Galaxy Watch 6. If the device is lost or stolen, this feature will prevent unauthorized users from accessing your sensitive information, such as text messages, health data, or payment methods. It also helps protect the watch from potential attacks by securing all digital contents on your device.

Activating the "Find My Watch" Feature in Case of Loss or Theft

The "Find My Watch" feature is an essential tool for locating your device if it's misplaced or stolen. It works by using your Samsung account to track the location of your Galaxy Watch 6. This feature not only helps you find your watch, but it also helps protect your data by remotely locking the device or wiping it clean if necessary.

How to Set Up "Find My Watch":

1. **Open Settings**: Swipe down from the top of the screen to access the **Quick Settings**, then tap on the **Settings** icon.

2. **Navigate to Security**: Scroll down and tap on **Security**.

3. **Select Find My Watch**: In the Security section, select the **Find My Watch** option. This will enable the feature that allows you to locate your device in case it's lost or stolen.

4. **Activate the Feature**: Toggle the switch to turn on **Find My Watch**. You will need to sign in to your **Samsung account** if you haven't already.

5. **Enable Remote Lock and Erase (Optional)**: You can also enable options to remotely lock your watch or erase its data if it's lost or stolen. These options are essential in ensuring that your personal data stays protected if someone else gains access to your watch.

Using "Find My Watch":

If your Galaxy Watch 6 goes missing, you can use the **Find My Watch** feature to locate it:

1. **Use the Samsung Wearable App**: Open the **Galaxy Wearable app** on your paired smartphone and select **Find My Watch**. The app will show you the last known location of your watch, and you can track its current location if it's within range.

2. **Play Sound**: If your watch is nearby, you can activate a sound alert to help you find it more easily.

3. **Lock or Erase Data**: If your watch is lost or stolen, you can remotely lock it using the **Find My Watch** feature. You can also choose to erase all data from the watch, preventing anyone from accessing your private information.

Data Privacy

With the Samsung Galaxy Watch 6, privacy is taken seriously. This smartwatch collects a range of data, including your activity, health, and fitness metrics, and it is important to understand how this data is used, stored, and shared. You also have control over your data privacy, including customizing privacy settings and choosing which data you wish to share.

How the Watch Collects and Stores Data (Health, Activity, etc.)

The Galaxy Watch 6 collects a wide variety of data to track your health, fitness, and daily activities. These include data related to your heart rate, steps, sleep patterns, exercise, and more. Additionally, the watch collects information about your movement and other lifestyle activities, such as your location for GPS-enabled workouts.

Types of Data Collected:

1. **Health Data**: The Galaxy Watch 6 tracks metrics like heart rate, blood pressure, ECG, SpO2 levels, and body composition. This data helps you monitor your overall health and fitness levels, offering insights into how well you're managing your well-being.

2. **Activity Data**: Your daily step count, calories burned, exercise routines, and activity levels are recorded and synced with the **Samsung Health app**. This helps you track your progress over time and maintain a healthy lifestyle.

3. **Location Data**: For outdoor activities like running, cycling, and hiking, the watch uses GPS to track your route and distance. This data is useful for workout analysis, but it's also sensitive because it involves your physical location.

4. **Sleep Data**: The watch monitors your sleep stages, quality, and duration. This data is stored in the **Samsung Health app** and helps you optimize your sleep patterns for better rest and recovery.

Where the Data Is Stored:

Samsung takes great care in storing your data securely. The majority of your data is stored in **Samsung's cloud services**, specifically in **Samsung Health** and **Samsung Cloud** (if enabled). These cloud services use encryption to protect your data from unauthorized access.

1. **Local Storage**: Some health and fitness data may be stored directly on the Galaxy Watch 6 itself, particularly if it's not synced with the cloud.

2. **Cloud Storage**: For a more comprehensive view of your health and fitness journey, your data is synced to the Samsung Cloud, where it can be accessed on other Samsung devices through your Samsung account.

Customizing Privacy Settings to Control Data Sharing and Storage

Samsung offers various settings that allow you to control what data is shared, with whom, and how it's used. You have the ability to manage your data privacy and make informed decisions about what information you wish to share with apps, third parties, or Samsung services.

How to Manage Privacy Settings:

1. **Open Settings**: Swipe down from the top of the watch screen to open the **Quick Settings** menu, then tap **Settings**.

2. **Navigate to Privacy**: Scroll down and tap on **Privacy** in the settings menu. Here, you'll find a variety of options to manage your privacy preferences.

3. **Control Data Sharing**:

    o **Health Data**: Under the **Samsung Health app**, you can choose which data you wish to share with other Samsung devices or third-party apps. For instance, you can disable sharing health data with fitness apps like Strava or MyFitnessPal if you prefer to keep it private.

    o **Location Data**: You can also control whether or not location data is shared during activities like running or hiking. In the **Privacy** settings, you can toggle off location tracking for apps that don't require it.

o **Third-Party Data Sharing**: Some apps may request access to certain data, such as health metrics or activity data. You can manage which apps are allowed to access this data in the **Permissions** section of the **Privacy** menu.

4. **Delete Data**:

   o If you no longer wish to store certain data on your Galaxy Watch 6 or Samsung Cloud, you can delete it. In the **Samsung Health app**, you can delete specific data records like workout history, health stats, or sleep data.

   o To delete data from Samsung Cloud, go to **Settings > Accounts and Backup > Samsung Cloud**, and select **Manage Storage** to delete unwanted data.

Understanding Samsung's Privacy Policies and Data Protection Measures

Samsung is committed to protecting your personal data and ensuring your privacy. The company adheres to strict **data protection** policies and practices, in compliance with global data protection laws such as the **General Data Protection**

Regulation (GDPR) and **California Consumer Privacy Act (CCPA)**. Understanding these policies is crucial for making informed decisions about data sharing.

Data Protection Measures:

1. **Encryption**: All sensitive data on your Galaxy Watch 6, including health information, is encrypted both during transmission (when synced with your smartphone or cloud services) and while stored on the device or in the cloud.

2. **Secure Connections**: Samsung uses **secure sockets layer (SSL)** and **encrypted communication protocols** to protect your data during transfer. This ensures that no third party can intercept or tamper with your information.

3. **Access Controls**: Samsung's privacy policy outlines who can access your data. By default, only you can access your personal data unless you explicitly grant access to third-party apps or services.

Samsung Privacy Policy Overview:

Samsung's privacy policy provides transparency on how your data is collected, used, and shared. Here's a summary of key aspects:

1. **Data Collection**: Samsung collects data to improve user experience, enhance services, and deliver personalized content. Data collection can be voluntary (such as when you enter personal information) or automatic (such as when tracking health metrics).

2. **Data Usage**: The data you share with Samsung may be used to personalize your services, improve health recommendations, and provide tailored advertising. You have control over the amount of data you share with third-party apps.

3. **Data Sharing**: Samsung does not sell your personal data. However, it may share certain anonymized data with third-party partners for service improvements, research, or advertising purposes. You can opt-out of certain data-sharing practices through privacy settings.

4. **Data Retention and Deletion**: Samsung retains your data only for as long as necessary to provide the services you've requested. You have the option to delete your data, either through the device or by contacting Samsung support.

The Samsung Galaxy Watch 6 offers an impressive array of security and privacy features that empower you to take control of your personal information. From securing your device with a PIN or password to using the "Find My Watch" feature in case of loss or theft, Samsung ensures that your data is protected every step of the way. Additionally, the ability to manage your privacy settings and understand how your data is used and stored gives you the peace of mind that your personal information is in safe hands.

By setting up secure locks, customizing data-sharing preferences, and staying informed about Samsung's privacy policies, you can enjoy the convenience and functionality of the Galaxy Watch 6 without compromising your privacy. As with all technology, it's important to regularly review and update your privacy settings to ensure they align with your comfort level. With Samsung's robust security and data protection measures, you can rest assured that your Galaxy Watch 6 is both a reliable and secure companion.

CHAPTER 8

Troubleshooting and Maintenance for the Samsung Galaxy Watch 6

Owning a Samsung Galaxy Watch 6 provides you with a powerful wearable device that enhances your daily life by offering fitness tracking, notifications, and connectivity on your wrist. However, like all electronic devices, it may occasionally experience issues that could disrupt your user experience. Whether it's connectivity problems, lagging performance, or software glitches, knowing how to troubleshoot and maintain your Galaxy Watch 6 will ensure that you can resolve these problems and keep your watch running smoothly. This chapter will guide you through common troubleshooting solutions and maintenance tips to help you get the most out of your device, ensuring its longevity and peak performance.

Common Issues and Fixes

While the Samsung Galaxy Watch 6 is a well-built device, users may encounter some issues from time to time. Fortunately, most of these problems are easy to resolve with a few simple steps. In this section, we'll go over common issues you may face, such as pairing problems, connectivity issues, lagging performance, software bugs, app crashes, and how to fix them.

Addressing Pairing Problems, Connectivity Issues, or Lagging Performance

One of the most common problems with smartwatches is difficulty pairing the device with your smartphone or connectivity issues. Additionally, lagging performance can be a frustrating issue that hinders your experience with the Galaxy Watch 6.

Pairing Problems:

Sometimes, users may experience difficulty pairing their Galaxy Watch 6 with a smartphone, which can occur due to Bluetooth interference, outdated software, or incorrect settings. Here's how you can resolve pairing issues:

1. **Ensure Bluetooth is On**: Ensure that Bluetooth is enabled on both your Galaxy Watch 6 and the smartphone. Go to your phone's **Bluetooth settings** and verify that Bluetooth is turned on. Also, make sure the watch is in pairing mode.

2. **Restart Both Devices**: If the devices are not pairing, try restarting both your Galaxy Watch 6 and your

smartphone. This can resolve any temporary software glitches or connection errors.

3. **Clear Previous Pairings**: If your watch has previously been paired with another device, it may cause interference. Go to the **Bluetooth settings** on your watch, and remove any previous pairings. Then, try pairing your Galaxy Watch 6 with your phone again.

4. **Use the Galaxy Wearable App**: Ensure that you have the **Galaxy Wearable** app installed on your smartphone. This app is essential for syncing your Galaxy Watch 6 and managing settings. Open the app and follow the on-screen instructions to pair your devices. If you're using an iPhone, ensure that the app is installed from the **App Store**.

5. **Check for Software Updates**: Ensure both your Galaxy Watch 6 and the Galaxy Wearable app are running the latest software versions. Outdated software can cause compatibility issues. Go to **Settings > Software Update** on your watch to check for and install updates.

Connectivity Issues:

Connectivity issues are also common when your Galaxy Watch 6 is not syncing properly with your smartphone or when there's trouble connecting to Wi-Fi, LTE, or Bluetooth.

1. **Wi-Fi and Bluetooth Connections**: If your Galaxy Watch 6 is not connecting to Wi-Fi or Bluetooth, check the Wi-Fi settings on the watch to ensure it's connected to the correct network. Go to **Settings > Connections > Wi-Fi** to select the correct network. For Bluetooth, ensure that the device is paired properly by opening the **Galaxy Wearable app**.

2. **Network Settings**: If your watch uses LTE, make sure the carrier's network is active and that your LTE plan is set up correctly. Check the **Samsung Health Monitor app** or the **Mobile Networks** settings in the **Galaxy Wearable app** for troubleshooting LTE connections.

3. **Disable Battery Saving Features**: Sometimes, battery-saving features like **Power Saving Mode** can limit connectivity. If you're experiencing connectivity issues, disable Power Saving Mode by

going to **Settings > Battery > Power Saving Mode** and ensuring it's turned off.

Lagging Performance:

Lagging performance can occur for a variety of reasons, including too many apps running in the background, insufficient available storage, or software bugs. Here's how to fix it:

1. **Close Unused Apps**: If you notice lagging, try closing unused apps running in the background. Press and hold the **Back button** to open the recent apps screen, then swipe away the apps that are not in use.

2. **Free Up Storage**: If your Galaxy Watch 6 is running low on storage, it may experience performance issues. Delete unnecessary files, such as old workout data, photos, or apps you no longer use. You can manage storage under **Settings > Storage**.

3. **Restart Your Watch**: Sometimes, a simple restart is the best solution to fix lagging performance. Restart your Galaxy Watch 6 by holding down the **Power button** and selecting **Restart**.

How to Reset Your Watch to Factory Settings

If the troubleshooting steps above don't solve the issue, performing a factory reset can often resolve persistent problems, such as software bugs or app crashes. A factory reset restores your watch to its original settings and erases all your personal data, so it's important to back up your information before proceeding.

Steps for Factory Reset:

1. **Go to Settings**: On your Galaxy Watch 6, swipe down to open the **Quick Settings**, then tap **Settings**.

2. **Navigate to Reset**: Scroll down to **General** and select **Reset**. You will be prompted to confirm the action.

3. **Confirm the Reset**: Once you confirm, the watch will begin the factory reset process. The device will erase all data, apps, and settings and restart to its default state.

4. **Set Up the Watch Again**: After the reset, you'll need to go through the initial setup process again. Pair your watch with your smartphone, sign in to your Samsung account, and restore any necessary apps or data.

Regular Maintenance Tips

To ensure your Galaxy Watch 6 remains in optimal condition, regular maintenance is essential. Whether it's keeping the screen clean, managing battery health, or ensuring software is up to date, performing regular maintenance can extend the life of your device and keep it functioning like new. Here are some tips for maintaining your Galaxy Watch 6.

Cleaning and Maintaining Your Samsung Galaxy Watch 6

Proper cleaning and care are essential to ensure that your Galaxy Watch 6 remains in good condition and continues to function as expected.

Cleaning the Watch:

1. **Clean the Strap**: If your watch has a **silicone, leather, or metal strap**, regularly clean it to remove dirt, sweat, and oils that can build up over time. Use a soft cloth and mild soap with water to wipe down the strap. For metal or leather bands, avoid getting them too wet. You can use a dedicated leather cleaner for leather bands.

2. **Clean the Screen**: Use a microfiber cloth to wipe the screen of your Galaxy Watch 6. Avoid using paper towels, as they can scratch the screen. For stubborn dirt or smudges, slightly dampen the cloth with water or a screen-safe cleaning solution.

3. **Water Resistance**: The Galaxy Watch 6 has **5ATM water resistance**, meaning it can withstand submersion in up to 50 meters of water. However, it's still important to clean the watch after swimming or intense exercise to remove saltwater, chlorine, or sweat that can cause damage over time.

4. **Ports and Sensors**: Use a dry, soft brush or cloth to clean the charging contacts and sensors on the back of the watch. Dirt or dust on these parts can interfere with charging or heart rate sensor accuracy.

Tips for Keeping Your Watch in Top Condition

In addition to regular cleaning, there are several other practices that can help keep your Samsung Galaxy Watch 6 in top condition.

1. **Screen Protection**: The screen is one of the most vulnerable parts of your watch. To prevent scratches or cracks, consider using a **screen protector** or a

watch case. This is especially useful if you engage in activities that expose the watch to potential impacts or rough surfaces.

2. **Sweat Management**: If you wear your watch during workouts, especially those involving sweat, make sure to wipe it down regularly. Sweat can build up on the watch's surface, leading to skin irritation or potential damage to the internal components. Always remove your watch after intense workouts to allow it to dry.

3. **Avoid Extreme Temperatures**: Avoid exposing your Galaxy Watch 6 to extreme temperatures, such as leaving it in a hot car or in freezing conditions. Extreme temperatures can negatively impact the battery life and overall performance of your device.

4. **Wear It Properly**: Make sure to wear the Galaxy Watch 6 snugly on your wrist to ensure proper tracking of health metrics. A loose fit can affect the accuracy of sensors like the heart rate monitor and skin temperature sensor.

Keeping the Device Updated with Software Updates and Security Patches

Regularly updating the software on your Galaxy Watch 6 is one of the most important aspects of maintenance. Updates provide bug fixes, performance improvements, and new features that keep your device running smoothly and securely.

Checking for Software Updates:

1. **Manual Updates**: Go to **Settings > Software Update** on your watch and select **Download and Install** to check for available updates. If an update is available, your watch will begin downloading and installing it.

2. **Automatic Updates**: Enable **Automatic Software Updates** to ensure that your Galaxy Watch 6 always stays up-to-date. This option can be found under **Settings > Software Update > Auto Update**.

Security Patches:

Samsung regularly releases security patches to protect your watch from vulnerabilities and threats. Keeping your device up-to-date ensures that you're protected from security risks.

1. **Update Security Patches**: The **Samsung Security Updates** are typically rolled out monthly. These patches include fixes for known security vulnerabilities and enhancements to the overall safety of the device.

2. **Enable Auto Security Updates**: Just like software updates, you can enable **auto security updates** to ensure your watch remains secure with the latest fixes.

Maintaining your Samsung Galaxy Watch 6 and troubleshooting common issues is essential for ensuring its longevity and optimal performance. Whether you're experiencing pairing issues, lagging performance, or simply want to keep your watch clean and updated, following the steps outlined in this chapter will help you resolve issues and maintain your device in top condition.

From troubleshooting software bugs and resetting your watch to keeping it clean and applying regular software updates, these practices ensure that your Galaxy Watch 6 continues to perform at its best. Regular maintenance, proper care, and staying up to date with software improvements will ensure that your Galaxy Watch 6 remains a reliable and functional part of your daily life for years to come.

CHAPTER 9

Exploring Apps and Extras on the Samsung Galaxy Watch 6

The Samsung Galaxy Watch 6 is more than just a smartwatch—it's an extension of your smartphone that provides not only fitness tracking and health monitoring but also entertainment, productivity, and third-party app support. With access to a wide variety of apps from the **Galaxy Store**, music, audio, and popular third-party integrations, the Galaxy Watch 6 offers a comprehensive ecosystem that enhances your digital lifestyle.

In this chapter, we will explore the world of apps and extras on your Galaxy Watch 6, guiding you through the process of installing apps, managing them, syncing music and audio, and integrating third-party services. By understanding these features, you can optimize the functionality of your watch to fit your needs, whether you're using it for fitness, entertainment, or personal productivity.

Installing Apps from the Galaxy Store

One of the key features of the Galaxy Watch 6 is its compatibility with a vast array of apps available through the

Galaxy Store. These apps allow you to extend the functionality of your smartwatch beyond the built-in features, adding everything from fitness tracking to social media management.

How to Browse, Install, and Manage Apps on Your Samsung Galaxy Watch 6

Browsing Apps on the Galaxy Store:

1. **Open the Galaxy Store**: On your Galaxy Watch 6, press the **Home button** to go to the main screen. Swipe up or press the **Apps icon** to open the app menu. Find and tap the **Galaxy Store** app to open it.

2. **Explore Categories**: The Galaxy Store offers a variety of categories like **Health & Fitness**, **Productivity**, **Entertainment**, **Lifestyle**, and more. Tap on any category to explore apps tailored to that specific category.

3. **Search for Specific Apps**: If you have a particular app in mind, use the **search bar** at the top of the Galaxy Store to type in the app's name. You can also browse through the **Featured** section for popular apps or check out **Editor's Picks** for app recommendations.

4. **App Details**: When you find an app that interests you, tap on it to view more details. This screen will show a description of the app, its features, and any ratings and reviews from other users. Be sure to check the **compatibility requirements** to ensure the app will work with your Galaxy Watch 6.

Installing Apps:

1. **Install the App**: Once you've found the app you want to install, tap the **Install** button. The app will download and install on your Galaxy Watch 6.

2. **Automatic Sync with Your Phone**: If the app is also available on your **smartphone**, you may be prompted to install it on your phone as well. For certain apps, syncing between your phone and watch enhances functionality, such as music streaming or fitness tracking.

3. **Permissions**: Some apps may request certain permissions to access data like your location, health information, or contacts. You can choose to accept or deny these permissions based on your preferences.

4. **Manage Installed Apps**: After installation, you can manage your apps from the **Apps menu** on your

watch. To uninstall an app, simply press and hold the app's icon, select **Uninstall**, and confirm the action.

Managing Installed Apps:

1. **Update Apps**: Just like your smartphone, apps on your Galaxy Watch 6 need regular updates to fix bugs, improve features, and stay compatible with new software updates. To check for updates, open the **Galaxy Store** and tap on the **Menu icon** (three horizontal lines), then go to **My Apps**. Here, you'll see a list of apps with available updates.

2. **App Settings**: Many apps have their own settings or preferences that can be customized. Access the app's settings either through the app itself or via the **Galaxy Wearable app** on your smartphone to fine-tune features such as notifications, layout, or syncing options.

Recommended Apps for Productivity, Fitness, and Entertainment

The Galaxy Store has a wide selection of apps designed to enhance various aspects of your life. Below are some of the most recommended apps for productivity, fitness, and entertainment that you can install on your Galaxy Watch 6:

Productivity Apps:

1. **Samsung Notes**: With the **Samsung Notes** app, you can create, view, and manage notes directly from your wrist. This app allows for quick note-taking, reminders, and lists while you're on the go.

2. **Microsoft Outlook**: If you use **Microsoft Outlook** for email, calendar, and tasks, you can install the Outlook app on your Galaxy Watch 6. This app lets you manage emails, calendar events, and reminders directly from the watch, keeping you organized throughout the day.

3. **Google Keep**: **Google Keep** is another great app for productivity, offering easy-to-use note-taking and checklist features. You can set reminders, save quick ideas, and sync your notes with other Google services.

Fitness Apps:

1. **Strava**: For cyclists, runners, and other outdoor fitness enthusiasts, **Strava** is an essential app. It tracks your workouts, provides detailed performance analytics, and allows you to share your results with friends and the Strava community.

2. **MyFitnessPal**: **MyFitnessPal** is perfect for tracking your nutrition and exercise goals. It can be synced with your Galaxy Watch 6 to log your daily activities, meals, and weight loss progress.

3. **Sleep Cycle**: Sleep tracking is an essential part of health, and **Sleep Cycle** helps you analyze your sleep patterns. It provides insights into sleep quality and tips on improving your sleep.

Entertainment Apps:

1. **Spotify**: **Spotify** on your Galaxy Watch 6 lets you control music playback, browse playlists, and even listen to music directly from your watch (when paired with Bluetooth headphones or speakers). You can also download music for offline listening.

2. **Audible**: If you enjoy audiobooks, **Audible** is a great app to install on your Galaxy Watch 6. You can listen to your favorite books while on the go, all without needing your phone nearby.

3. **YouTube Music**: If you're subscribed to **YouTube Premium**, you can also use **YouTube Music** on your Galaxy Watch 6 to stream your favorite music, podcasts, and playlists directly from your wrist.

Using Music and Audio on Your Watch

Listening to music, podcasts, or audiobooks on your Galaxy Watch 6 is an excellent way to stay entertained while on the go. Whether you're working out, commuting, or just relaxing, your watch can double as a portable media player. Let's explore how to sync your favorite content to the watch and enjoy high-quality audio with Bluetooth headphones.

Syncing Music, Podcasts, and Audiobooks to Your Device

The Galaxy Watch 6 allows you to sync various forms of audio content, including music, podcasts, and audiobooks, directly to your device. This is particularly useful if you want to leave your phone behind during a run or workout but still want to enjoy your media.

Syncing Music:

1. **Use the Music App**: The default music player app on your Galaxy Watch 6 allows you to sync and play music directly from your device. To start, open the **Music** app on your watch, then tap **Add Music**. From there, you can sync music files from your smartphone, or if you use a music streaming service

like **Spotify** or **YouTube Music**, you can log in and download playlists or albums to your watch for offline listening.

2. **Use Samsung Galaxy Wearable App**: The **Galaxy Wearable app** allows you to manage the music on your watch. Under the **Music** section, you can choose which music to sync from your phone to the watch. It supports a wide range of formats like MP3, AAC, and WAV.

Syncing Podcasts and Audiobooks:

1. **Spotify Podcasts**: For Spotify users, podcasts are available directly within the Spotify app on your Galaxy Watch 6. Simply search for your favorite podcasts and download episodes for offline listening.

2. **Audible Audiobooks**: If you enjoy audiobooks, you can sync them from the **Audible** app to your watch. After installing the Audible app on both your phone and your watch, simply choose the audiobooks you want to download and listen to directly from your wrist.

3. **Pocket Casts**: Another excellent podcast app is **Pocket Casts**. You can sync your podcast

subscriptions and listen to your favorite shows without needing your phone.

Using Bluetooth Headphones to Enjoy Audio While on the Go

One of the key features of listening to music and audio on your Galaxy Watch 6 is the ability to pair it with Bluetooth headphones or speakers. This allows you to enjoy media without the need for your phone.

Pairing Bluetooth Headphones:

1. **Enable Bluetooth**: On your Galaxy Watch 6, swipe down from the top of the screen to open **Quick Settings**. Ensure that Bluetooth is enabled.

2. **Pairing the Headphones**: Open the **Bluetooth settings** on your Galaxy Watch 6. Tap **Search for Devices**, then put your Bluetooth headphones in pairing mode. Once your headphones appear, select them to pair with your watch.

3. **Adjusting Volume**: Once paired, you can control the volume directly from the watch or adjust it on your headphones.

4. **Listen on the Go**: Whether you're running, walking, or just enjoying music at home, you can now enjoy high-quality audio directly from your Galaxy Watch 6.

Third-Party Integrations

One of the greatest strengths of the Samsung Galaxy Watch 6 is its ability to integrate with various third-party apps and services. This allows you to expand the functionality of your watch beyond Samsung's native apps. Whether it's tracking your fitness progress with **Google Fit**, syncing with **Strava** for running or cycling, or using **IFTTT** for automation, the Galaxy Watch 6 ensures you stay connected and productive.

Connecting Your Watch to Google Fit, Strava, and Other Popular Apps

The Galaxy Watch 6 allows you to integrate with several popular third-party fitness apps, making it a flexible device for fitness enthusiasts and anyone who wants to track their health and activity seamlessly.

Integrating with Google Fit:

1. **Download Google Fit**: Install the **Google Fit** app on your Galaxy Watch 6 by visiting the **Galaxy Store**.

Once installed, open the app and sign in with your Google account.

2. **Sync Data**: Google Fit syncs various health metrics like steps, heart rate, and calories burned. You can now track your activity in Google Fit, alongside Samsung Health.

3. **Track Workouts**: The Galaxy Watch 6 can track workouts using Google Fit's data, including running, walking, and cycling.

Integrating with Strava:

1. **Install Strava**: Download and install the **Strava** app on your watch via the **Galaxy Store**. Log in to your Strava account to sync your activity data.

2. **Track Runs and Rides**: The integration allows you to track runs and rides, providing accurate GPS data, pace, and cadence. Your workouts will sync with the Strava app, allowing you to view and analyze them in-depth.

Using IFTTT for Automation:

1. **Install IFTTT**: Use the **IFTTT** (If This Then That) app to automate tasks between your Galaxy Watch 6

and other devices. For instance, you can automate the process of logging daily activity into a Google Sheet or set up reminders based on your watch's GPS location.

2. **Set Up Triggers and Actions**: Create custom **applets** that trigger actions on your Galaxy Watch 6. For example, you can set up an applet to turn off your smart home lights when you leave your home or send a notification when you reach a fitness goal.

The Samsung Galaxy Watch 6 offers an exceptional range of apps and extras that make it more than just a wearable for fitness and notifications. By installing apps from the **Galaxy Store**, syncing music and audio for entertainment, and integrating with popular third-party apps like **Google Fit**, **Strava**, and **IFTTT**, the Galaxy Watch 6 enhances your lifestyle and helps you stay connected, productive, and entertained. With the right apps and integrations, your Galaxy Watch 6 becomes a powerful, personalized device that suits all your needs. Whether you're tracking workouts, listening to podcasts, or automating tasks, the Galaxy Watch 6 is equipped to support your every activity.

CONCLUSION

Making the Most of Your Samsung Galaxy Watch 6

As we wrap up this guide, it's time to reflect on the incredible capabilities of the **Samsung Galaxy Watch 6** and how you can continue to make the most of it moving forward. From its cutting-edge health and fitness features to seamless connectivity and versatility, the Galaxy Watch 6 is designed to fit effortlessly into your lifestyle, helping you stay organized, healthy, and connected. Let's take a moment to review the key features, understand how to use the watch consistently for maximum benefit, and look ahead to future possibilities with continued software updates and improvements.

A Recap of Key Features

The Samsung Galaxy Watch 6 is packed with features that not only enhance your day-to-day life but also help you achieve long-term health and productivity goals. Whether you're a fitness enthusiast, a busy professional, or someone who simply enjoys the convenience of a connected smartwatch, the Galaxy Watch 6 offers a wide array of functions that make it indispensable.

Health Monitoring and Fitness Tracking

One of the standout features of the Galaxy Watch 6 is its **comprehensive health monitoring tools**. From tracking your **heart rate**, **ECG**, **blood pressure**, and **SpO2 levels** to **sleep tracking**, **body composition analysis**, and **stress management**, this smartwatch takes your health and wellness seriously. The watch's ability to track a wide variety of metrics allows you to monitor your physical well-being with precision and makes it easier to set realistic goals based on real-time data.

For fitness enthusiasts, the **Galaxy Watch 6** supports numerous exercise modes, including **running**, **cycling**, **swimming**, **yoga**, and more. With built-in **GPS**, it can accurately track your routes and provide insights into your performance, such as pace, cadence, and heart rate zones. Whether you're training for a race, recovering from an injury, or simply trying to stay active, the Galaxy Watch 6 gives you the tools to monitor and improve your fitness levels.

Connectivity

The Galaxy Watch 6 is more than just a fitness tracker; it's a comprehensive communication tool. Whether you're at work or on the go, you can stay connected through **notifications, messages**, and **calls**. With the ability to **pair with your smartphone** or connect directly to **LTE**, you can make calls, send texts, and receive notifications directly from your wrist—no need to pull out your phone. Additionally, the watch syncs seamlessly with various apps like **Google Fit, Strava, Spotify**, and **Samsung SmartThings**, making it a hub for all your digital needs.

Customization and Personalization

The Galaxy Watch 6 allows you to express your style with **customizable watch faces**, as well as personalized settings to control everything from notifications to display options. Whether you prefer a minimalist design or something more detailed, you can adjust the appearance of the watch to suit your personal tastes. And with the ability to install third-party apps, you can tailor the watch even further to your needs, making it uniquely yours.

Encouraging Regular Use

To get the most out of your Samsung Galaxy Watch 6, regular use is key. The more consistently you use the watch, the better the insights and benefits you will gain from it. Let's explore how to integrate this device into your daily routine for maximum benefit.

How to Use the Watch Consistently for Maximum Benefit

To truly make the most of your Galaxy Watch 6, it's important to integrate it into your daily life, using it for both practical and personal purposes. Here are a few tips to help you maintain a consistent and effective use of your smartwatch:

1. **Wear It Every Day**: The Galaxy Watch 6 offers a range of health metrics that rely on continuous monitoring. By wearing it throughout the day, you'll be able to track your **step count**, **heart rate**, **sleep**, and other key health data. Consistent wear also ensures that you can get the most out of features like **activity reminders** and **fitness tracking**.

2. **Use It for Notifications**: Keep your watch paired to your phone so that you can receive notifications on

your wrist. This will help you stay on top of important calls, messages, and alerts without constantly reaching for your phone. Whether you're at work, exercising, or running errands, you'll never miss an important update.

3. **Track Your Health and Fitness**: Set regular health goals, whether it's achieving a specific number of steps per day, maintaining a target heart rate, or improving your sleep quality. The Galaxy Watch 6 offers real-time feedback that helps you stay on track. Set daily reminders for exercise, hydration, or even breathing exercises to ensure you're consistently working toward your health goals.

4. **Utilize Music and Audio**: Make use of the music, podcast, and audiobook capabilities to enjoy entertainment during workouts or commutes. By syncing your favorite playlists and podcasts to the watch, you can leave your phone at home while still enjoying your preferred audio content on the go.

5. **Customize Watch Faces and Settings**: With so many customization options available, you can make the Galaxy Watch 6 fit your personal style and needs. Whether it's choosing a watch face that matches your

outfit or adjusting settings to receive only the notifications you care about, personalized settings can help make your smartwatch a more seamless part of your routine.

Staying Up-to-Date with New Features via Updates

One of the best things about the Galaxy Watch 6 is that Samsung continually improves the watch's functionality and performance through software updates. These updates often include **new features**, **bug fixes**, and **security patches**, ensuring that your device remains up-to-date and fully functional.

To ensure you're always getting the latest features and improvements, make sure to:

1. **Enable Automatic Updates**: Go to **Settings > Software Update** on your Galaxy Watch 6 and turn on **Auto Update** to ensure that your device automatically downloads and installs the latest updates when available.

2. **Regularly Check for Updates**: Even with auto updates enabled, it's a good habit to check for updates manually every now and then. This is especially important if you experience any issues or

if you want to take advantage of newly released features.

3. **Review Update Notes**: After updating your Galaxy Watch 6, take a moment to review the **release notes** or **patch notes** that come with each update. This will keep you informed about new features or performance enhancements that Samsung has introduced.

Looking Ahead

While the **Samsung Galaxy Watch 6** is a highly capable device as it stands, Samsung is constantly working to improve and expand the capabilities of its smartwatches. Let's take a look at how you can future-proof your Galaxy Watch 6 experience and prepare for what lies ahead.

Future-Proofing Your Experience as Samsung Continues to Release New Features and Enhancements

Samsung has a proven track record of providing long-term software support for its Galaxy Watch line, and the Galaxy Watch 6 will no doubt benefit from continued updates and new features. Here's how you can stay ahead of the curve:

1. **Stay Engaged with Samsung's Ecosystem**: Samsung is likely to continue enhancing the

integration between the Galaxy Watch 6 and other devices within its ecosystem, such as **Samsung smartphones**, **tablets**, **SmartThings**, and **Samsung Health**. By keeping your device synced with the Samsung ecosystem, you'll be able to take full advantage of these improvements.

2. **Leverage Samsung's Health and Fitness Advancements**: As the healthcare and fitness industries evolve, Samsung is expected to add new health monitoring tools and features to the Galaxy Watch 6. This could include more accurate sensors, additional workout modes, and deeper integration with health apps. Keeping your device updated will ensure you don't miss out on these innovations.

3. **Keep an Eye on Compatibility with New Apps**: Samsung's **Galaxy Store** is constantly updated with new apps, and as developers create more watch-friendly applications, your Galaxy Watch 6 will only get more versatile. New third-party apps for fitness, productivity, and entertainment will continue to improve the functionality of your device.

4. **Prepare for Future Hardware Updates**: While the Galaxy Watch 6 is already packed with features,

Samsung frequently releases updated hardware models. Newer models may feature better sensors, improved performance, or more advanced battery technology. If you decide to upgrade in the future, the foundation you've built with the Galaxy Watch 6 will make transitioning to newer models even easier.

Enjoying a Smarter, Healthier, and More Productive Lifestyle with the Samsung Galaxy Watch 6

The Galaxy Watch 6 is not just a smartwatch—it's a tool that can help you lead a smarter, healthier, and more productive lifestyle. By integrating the watch into your daily routine and using it consistently, you'll be able to achieve better health, stay on top of your tasks, and remain connected no matter where life takes you. Here's how you can continue to make the most of your device:

1. **Track Your Health and Fitness Progress**: As you use your Galaxy Watch 6, keep track of your health metrics over time. Whether it's your heart rate, sleep quality, or exercise performance, the data collected by the watch will help you set goals and monitor your progress toward better health.

2. **Stay Connected**: With its ability to handle notifications, calls, and messages, the Galaxy Watch 6 helps you stay connected while keeping your hands free. Whether you're working, exercising, or spending time with loved ones, the watch ensures you don't miss important updates.

3. **Boost Your Productivity**: By using apps for task management, calendar events, reminders, and notes, you can boost your productivity and stay organized. The ability to access and manage your tasks directly from your wrist allows for a smoother, more efficient workflow throughout your day.

4. **Explore Entertainment on the Go**: Whether it's music, podcasts, or audiobooks, the Galaxy Watch 6 provides entertainment that's always at your fingertips. Sync your favorite content to the watch and enjoy high-quality audio while you work out or commute.

The **Samsung Galaxy Watch 6** is more than just a smartwatch—it's an all-in-one device that helps you stay fit, organized, and connected. By fully utilizing its health monitoring, fitness tracking, and connectivity features, you can improve your lifestyle and make the most of every day.

With regular use, staying up-to-date with software updates, and looking ahead to future features, the Galaxy Watch 6 will continue to serve as a valuable tool in your daily life.

As Samsung continues to enhance the Galaxy Watch series, you can rest assured that your Galaxy Watch 6 will remain a key part of your digital experience. Whether you're focused on health, productivity, or simply enjoying entertainment on the go, this smartwatch is ready to help you achieve a smarter, healthier, and more productive lifestyle.

www.ingramcontent.com/pod-product-compliance
Lightning Source LLC
La Vergne TN
LVHW051653050326
832903LV00032B/3785